How To Write Hebrew Alphabet (Alef-Bet)

Step By Step Workbook For Beginners
(Kids & Adults)
Learn How To Write Hebrew Letters

By Rachel Mintz

Created for Arad & Tomer
Who will soon learn to read & write

Copyright © 2017 Palm Tree Publishing - All rights reserved. No part of this publication may be reproduced, distributed, or transmitted in any form or by any means, including photocopying, recording, or other electronic or mechanical methods, without the prior written permission of the publisher, except in the case of brief quotations embodied in critical reviews and certain other noncommercial uses permitted by copyright law.

About This Book

With this book you will learn how to write Hebrew letters (Alef-Bet).

Learning the Hebrew ABC (Alef-Bet) is the first stage before you can begin to learn how to read Hebrew. Identifying the letters, and knowing how to write them will speed up your Hebrew lessons.

How To Use This Book

Say the name of the letters aloud.

Follow with a pen over the lines and dotted lines, keep practicing until you master writing letter.

Each time you write a letter say it loud so you will get triple learning – Recognizing the visual, writing the letter, hearing its name.

Do 3-4 letters per day, do not try and stuff everything too fast, allow yourself to absorb the new letters few at a time.

Practice & practice and practice some more..

Did You Know:

The Hebrew language was used 4000 years ago, by Abraham, Isiac and Jacob. It was used by Moses 3500 years ago when he spoke to the Children of Israel in Egypt.

King David used Hebrew 3000 years ago when he made Jerusalem the capital city of Israel, so did King Solomon who build the Jewish Temple on the Temple Mount in Jerusalem. Jesus was using Hebrew 2000 years ago too.

In Jerusalem and across Israel were found numerous scripts, scrolls, clay carving, stone decorations with Hebrew on them, dating back 3000 years.

In those days the Hebrew letters were written slightly different, and are called Ktav Ivri.

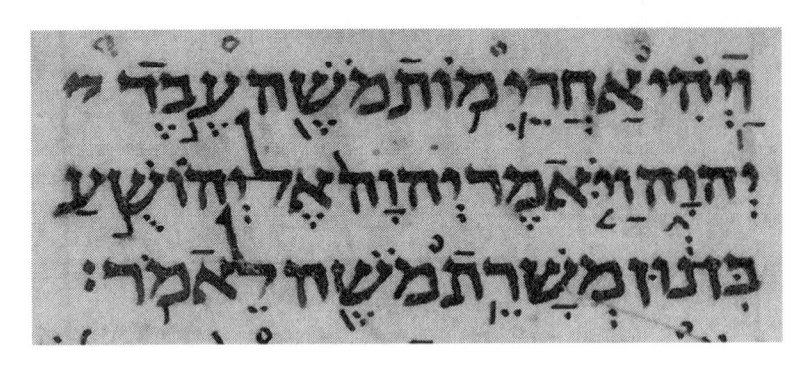

וַיְהִי אַחֲרֵי מוֹת מֹשֶׁה עֶבֶד יְהוָה וַיֹּאמֶר יְהוָה אֶל־יְהוֹשֻׁעַ בִּן־נוּן מְשָׁרֵת מֹשֶׁה לֵאמֹר

At 135 AD most of the Jewish people were deported from Israel by the Romans. The Romans who wanted to erase any trace of Jewish sovereignty changed the name of Judea to Palestina.

For 2000 years, Jews were living in dozens of foreign countries, using Hebrew language only for praying.

About 200 years ago, when the Russian pogroms began, Jews started to head back home and the Hebrew language was revived. Today it is the official language in Israel.

There are 22 letters in the Hebrew Alphabet + 5 Final form letters which are written differently when they are at the end of a word.

Hebrew is written and read from RIGHT to left.

Read The Alef Bet

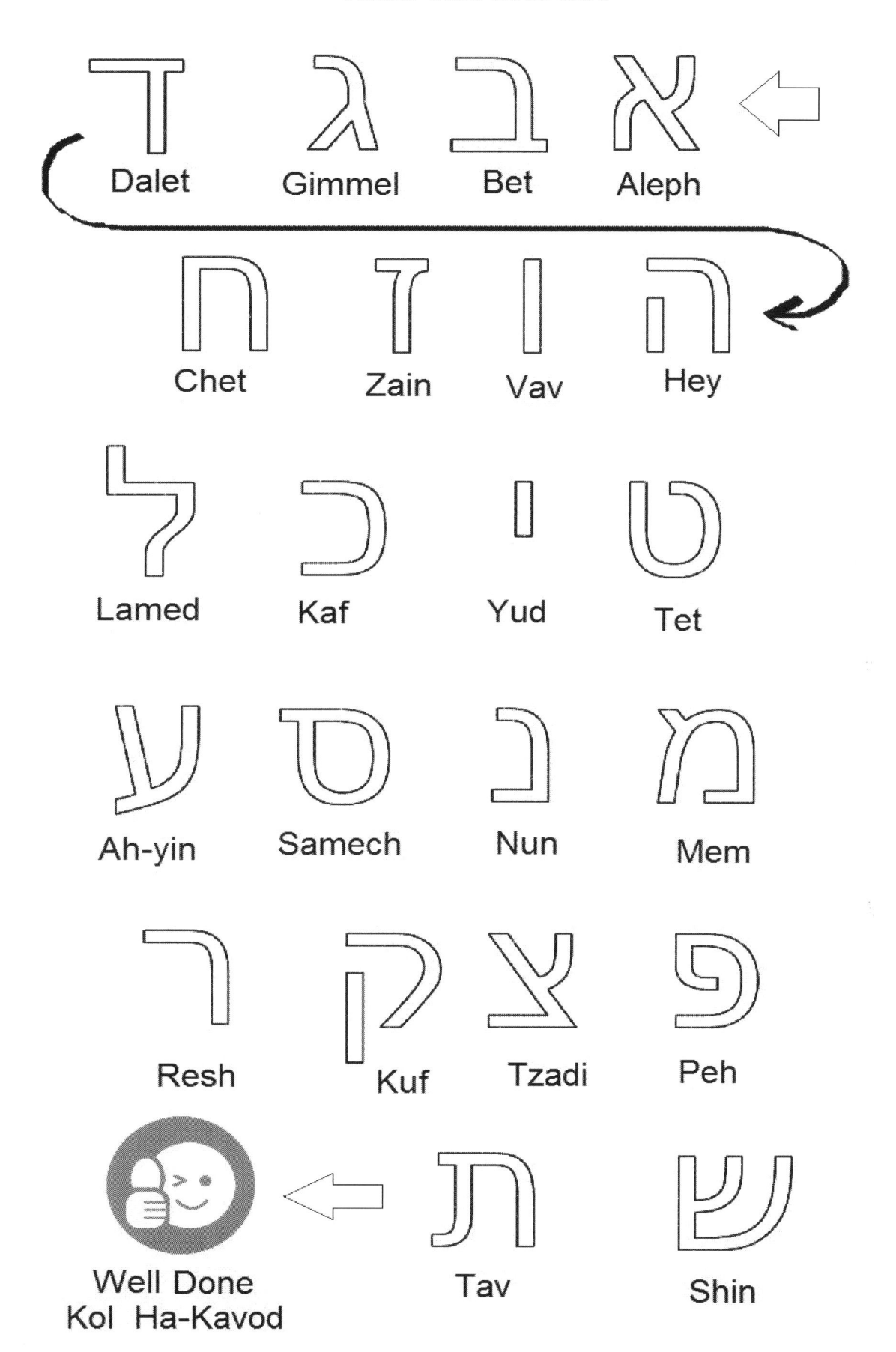

| ד Dalet | ג Gimmel | ב Bet | א Aleph |

| ח Chet | ז Zain | ו Vav | ה Hey |

| ל Lamed | כ Kaf | י Yud | ט Tet |

| ע Ah-yin | ס Samech | נ Nun | מ Mem |

| ר Resh | ק Kuf | צ Tzadi | פ Peh |

| Well Done Kol Ha-Kavod | ת Tav | ש Shin |

Now let's begin to learn to write the Alef-Bet

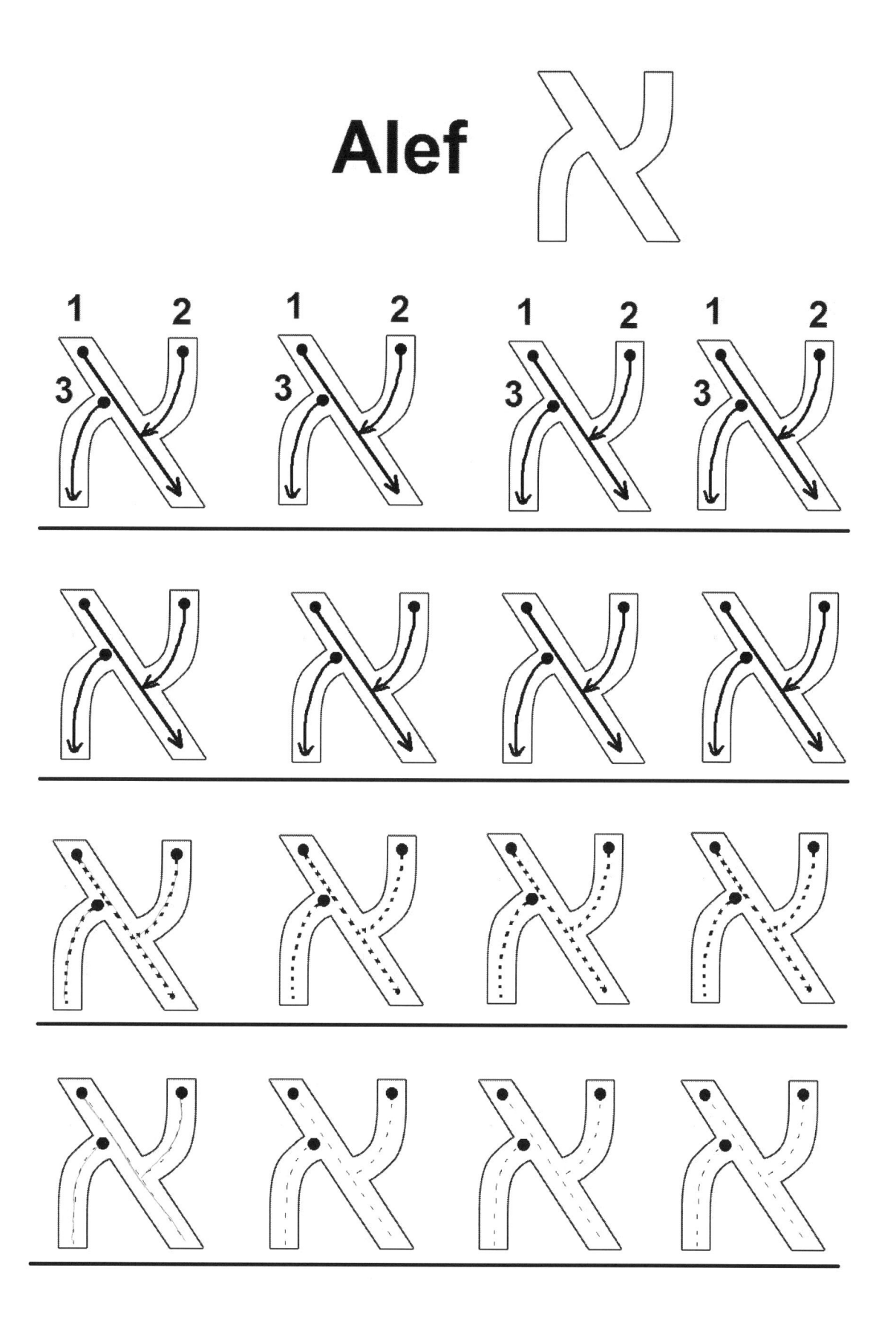

Alef א

Alef א

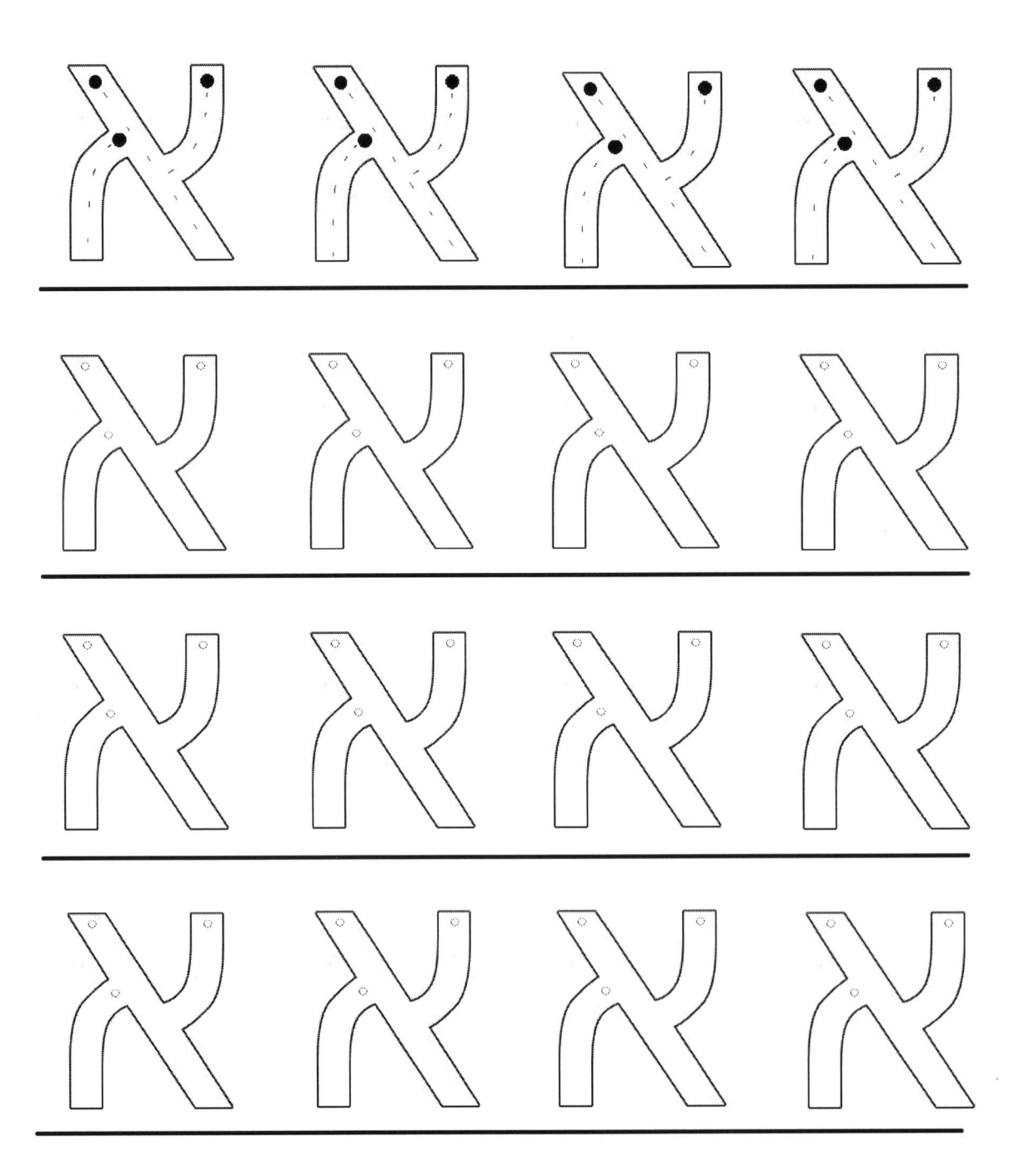

Alef א

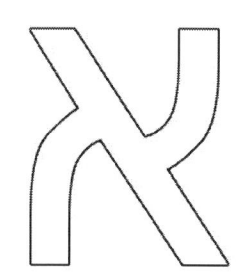

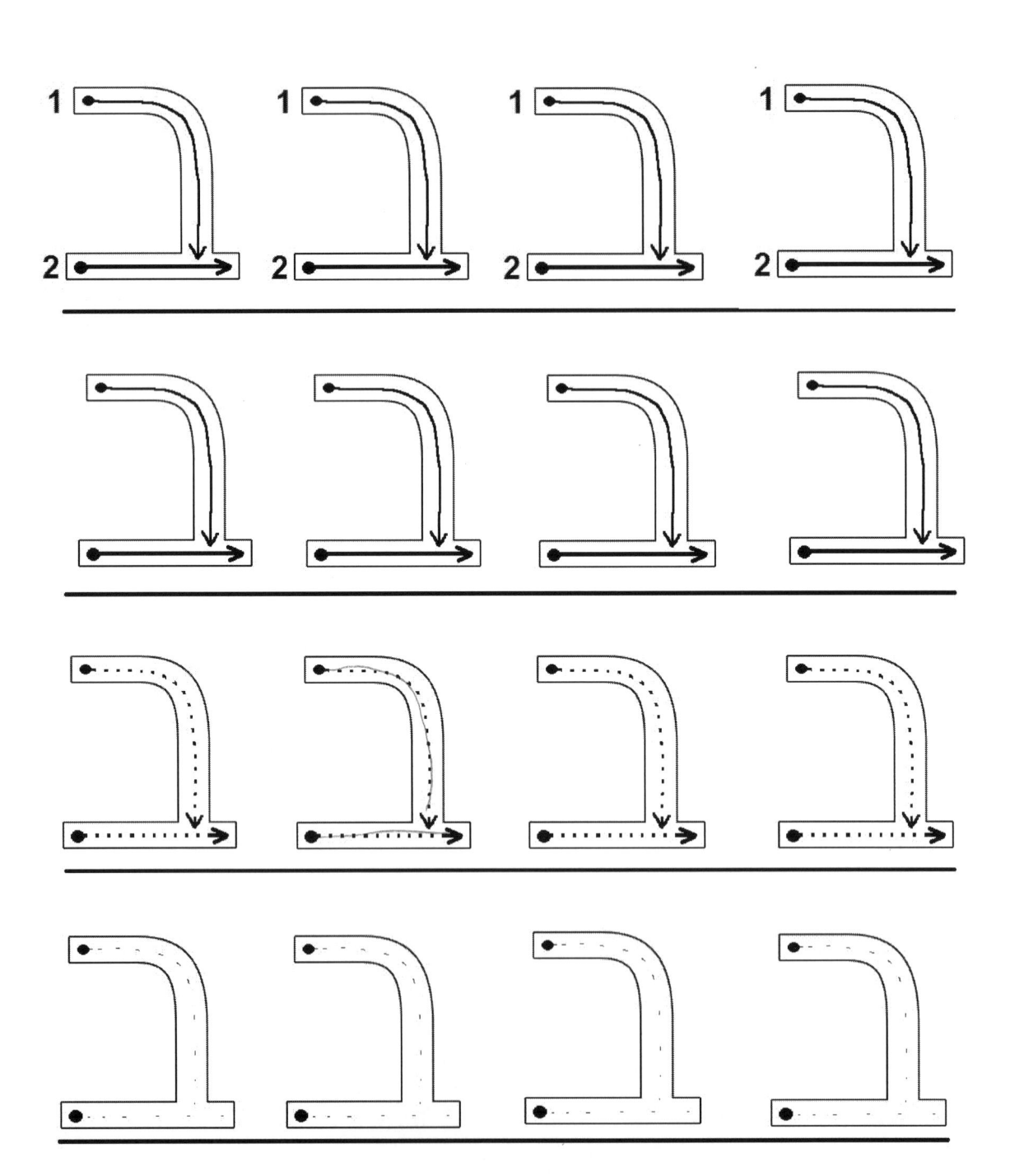

Bet

Bet ב

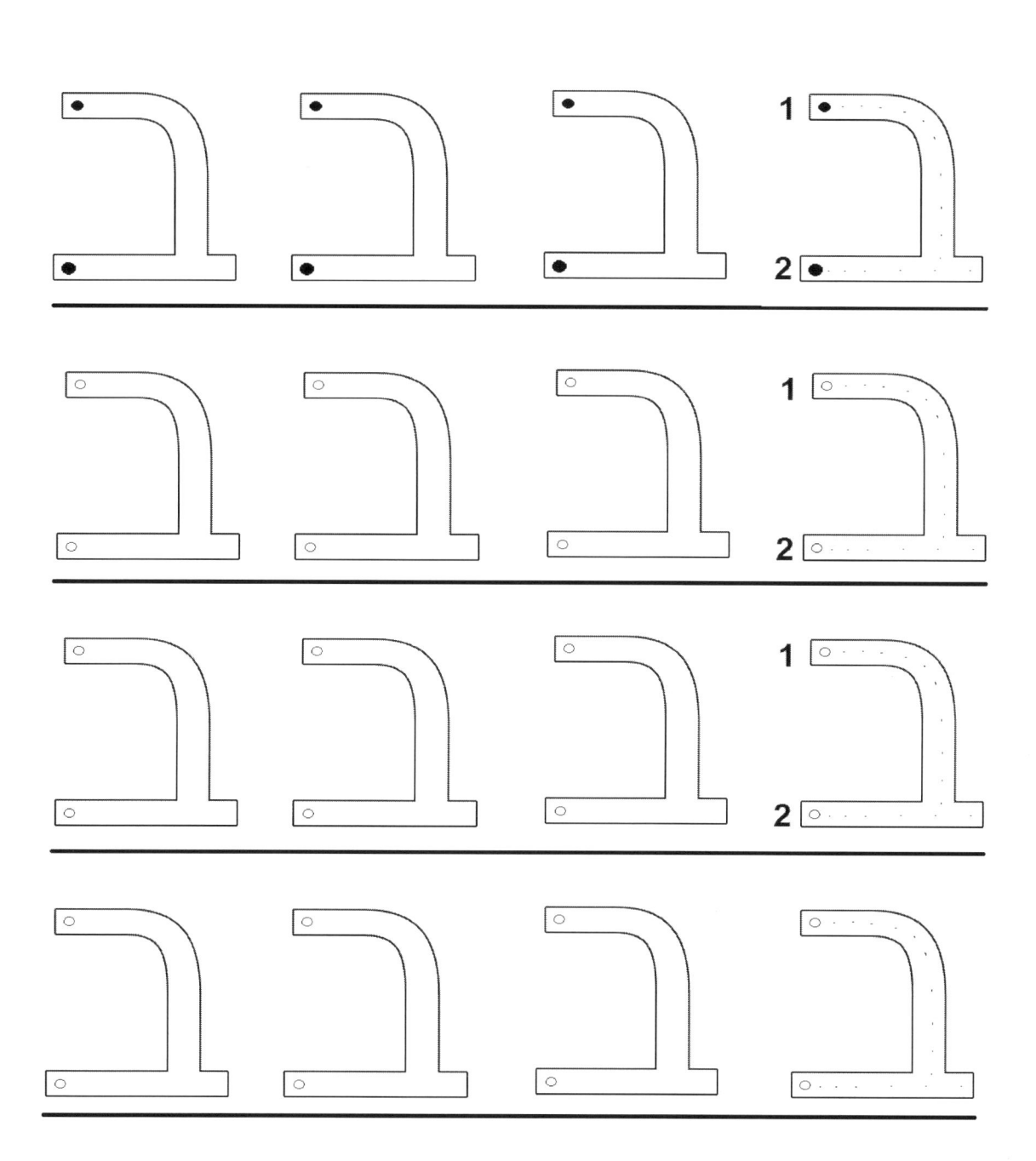

Bet ב

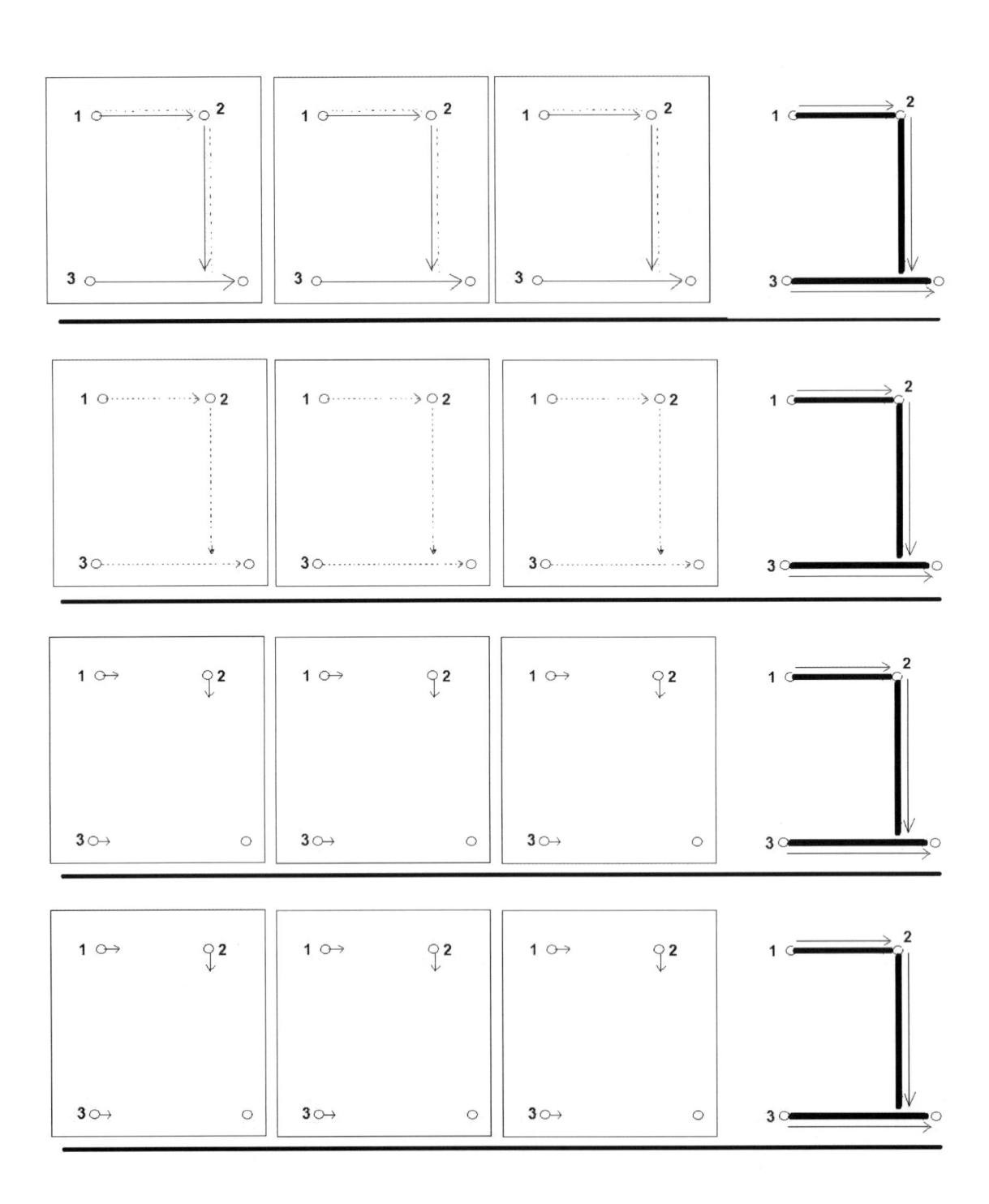

Bet ב

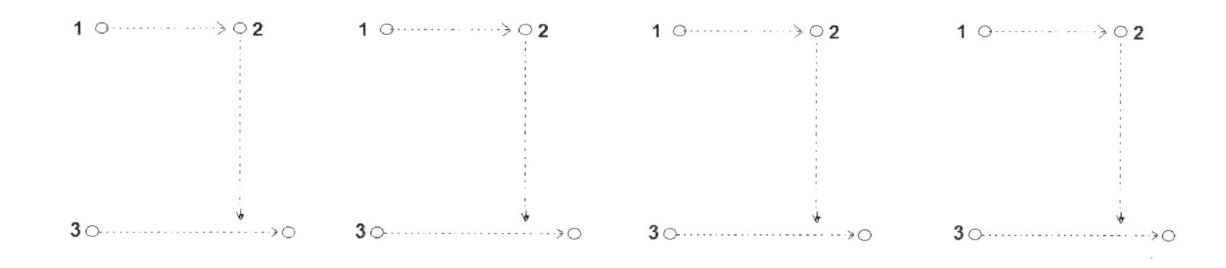

Gimel

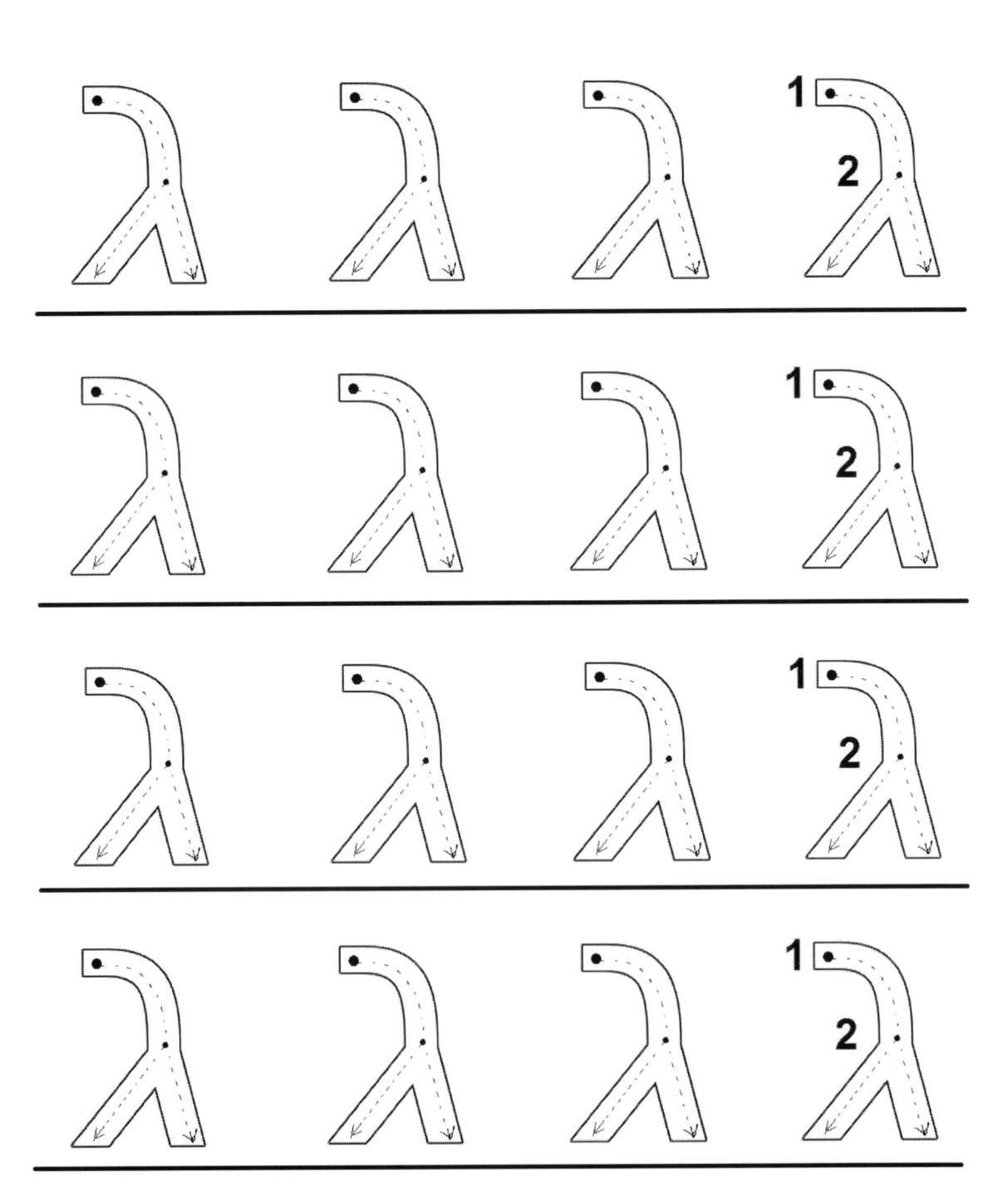

Gimel ג

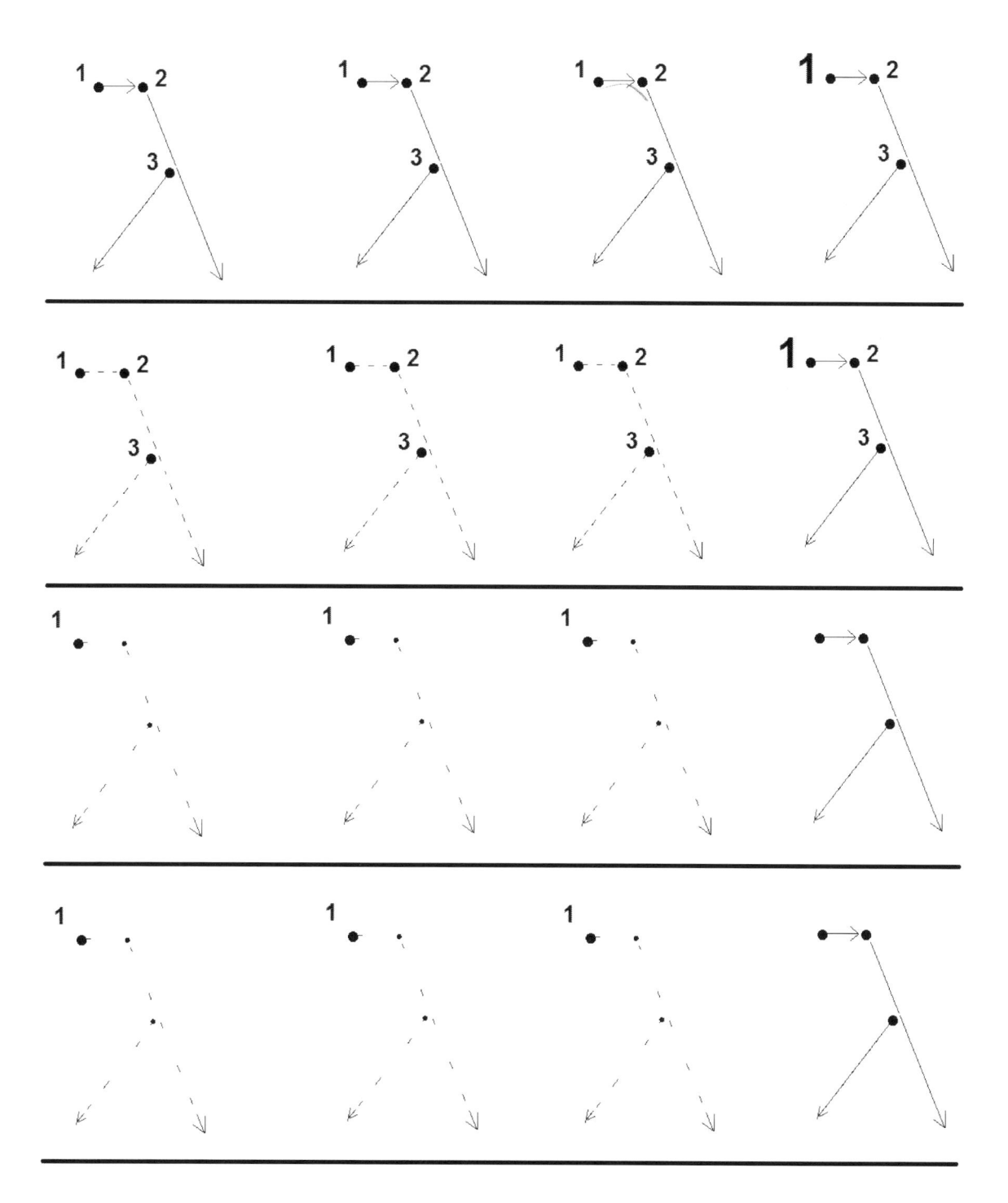

Gimel ג

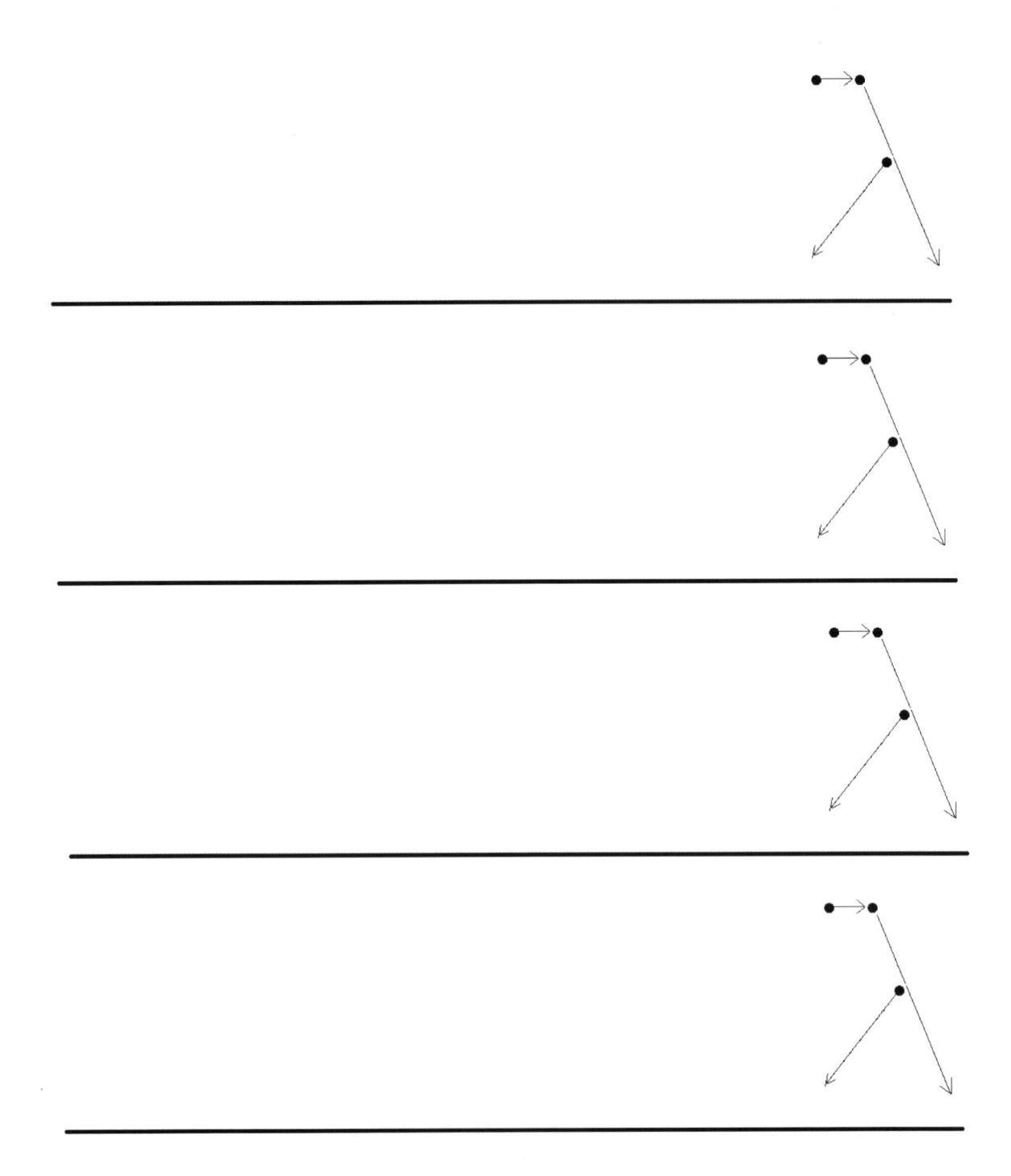

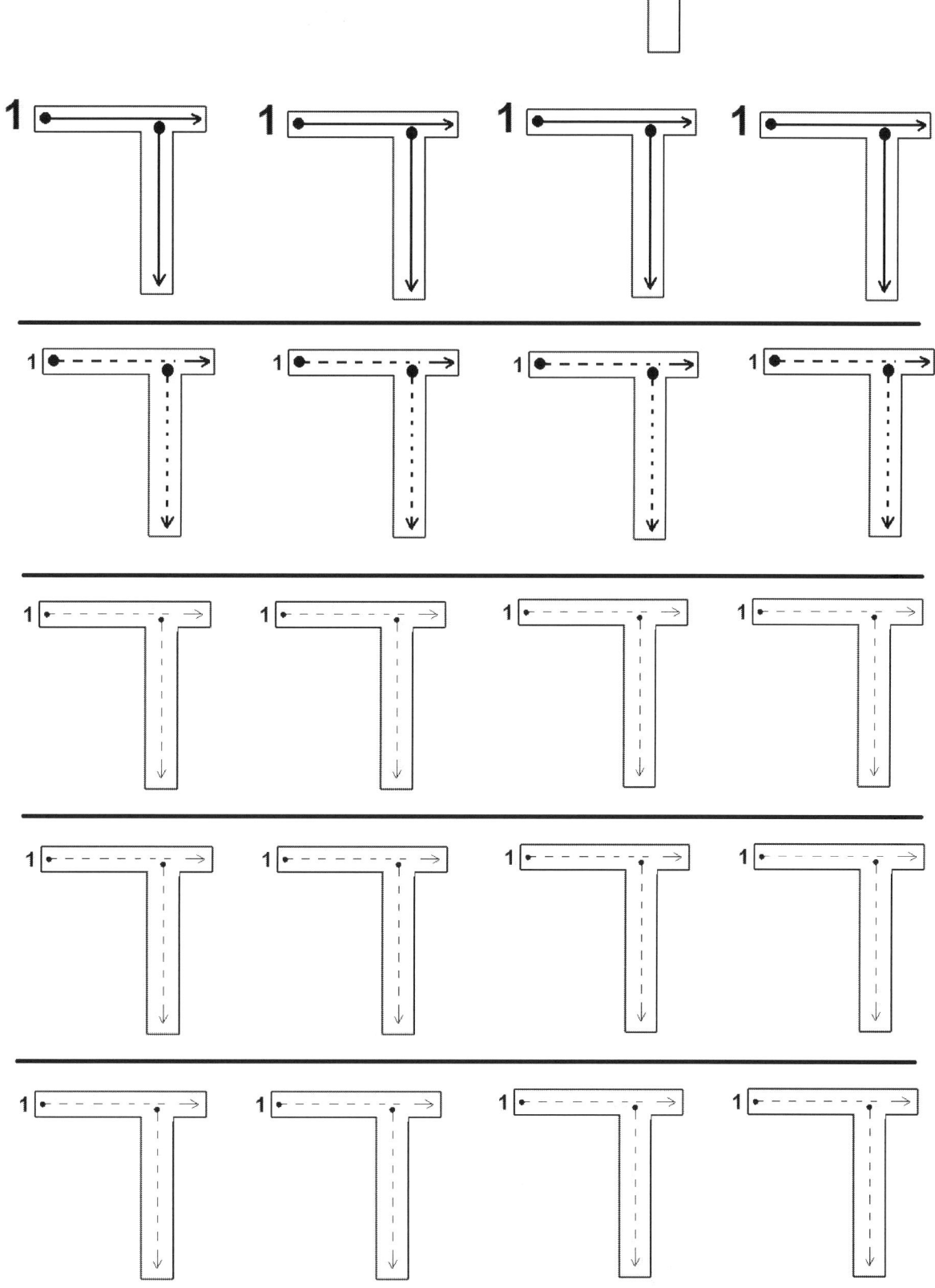

Dalet

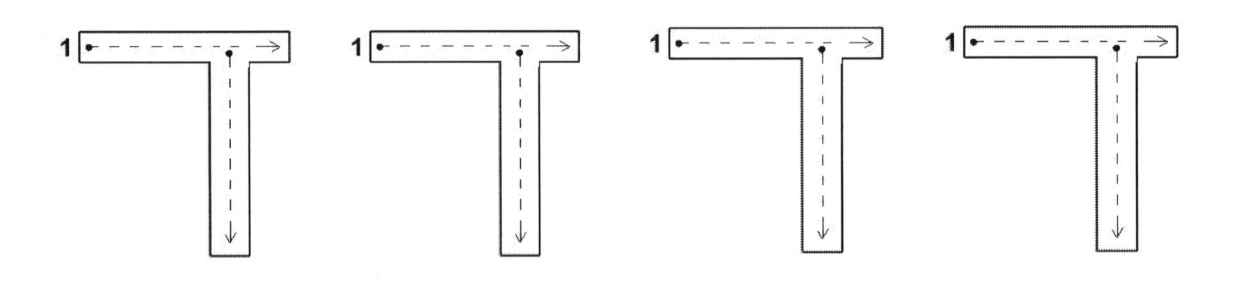

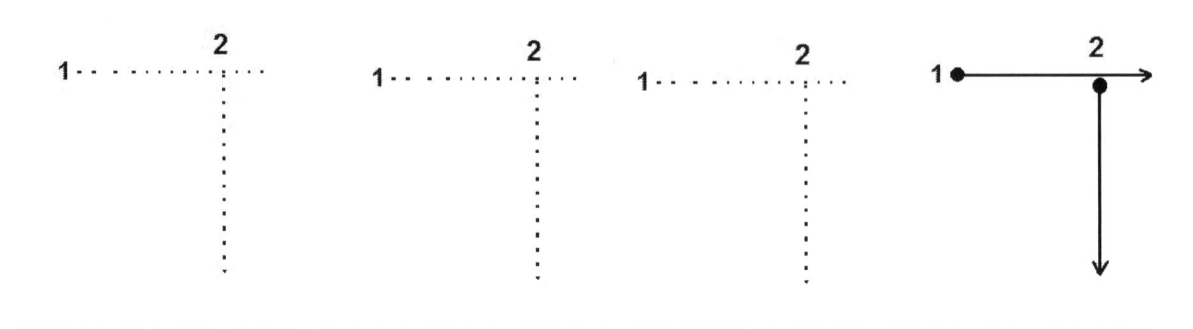

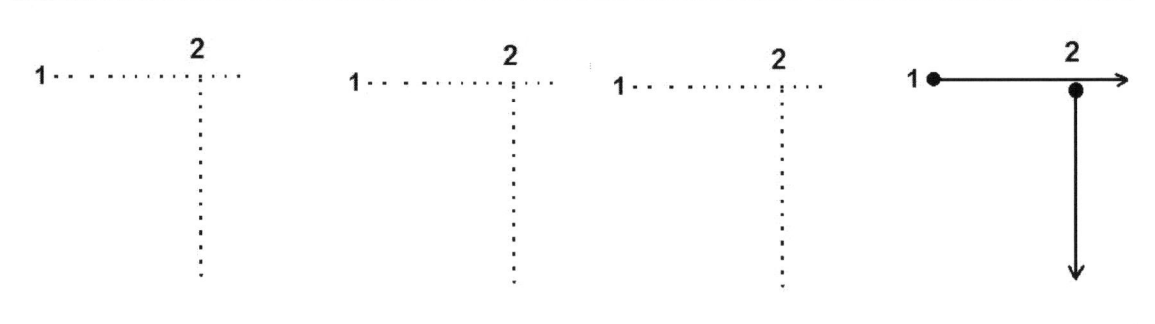

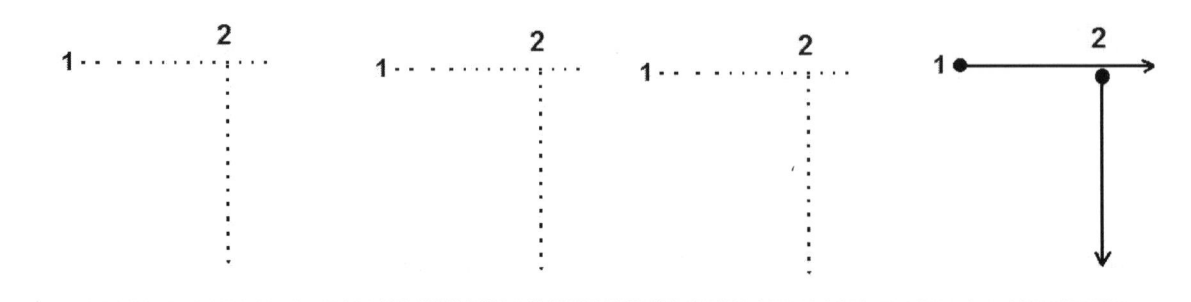

Dalet

Dalet T

Hey ה

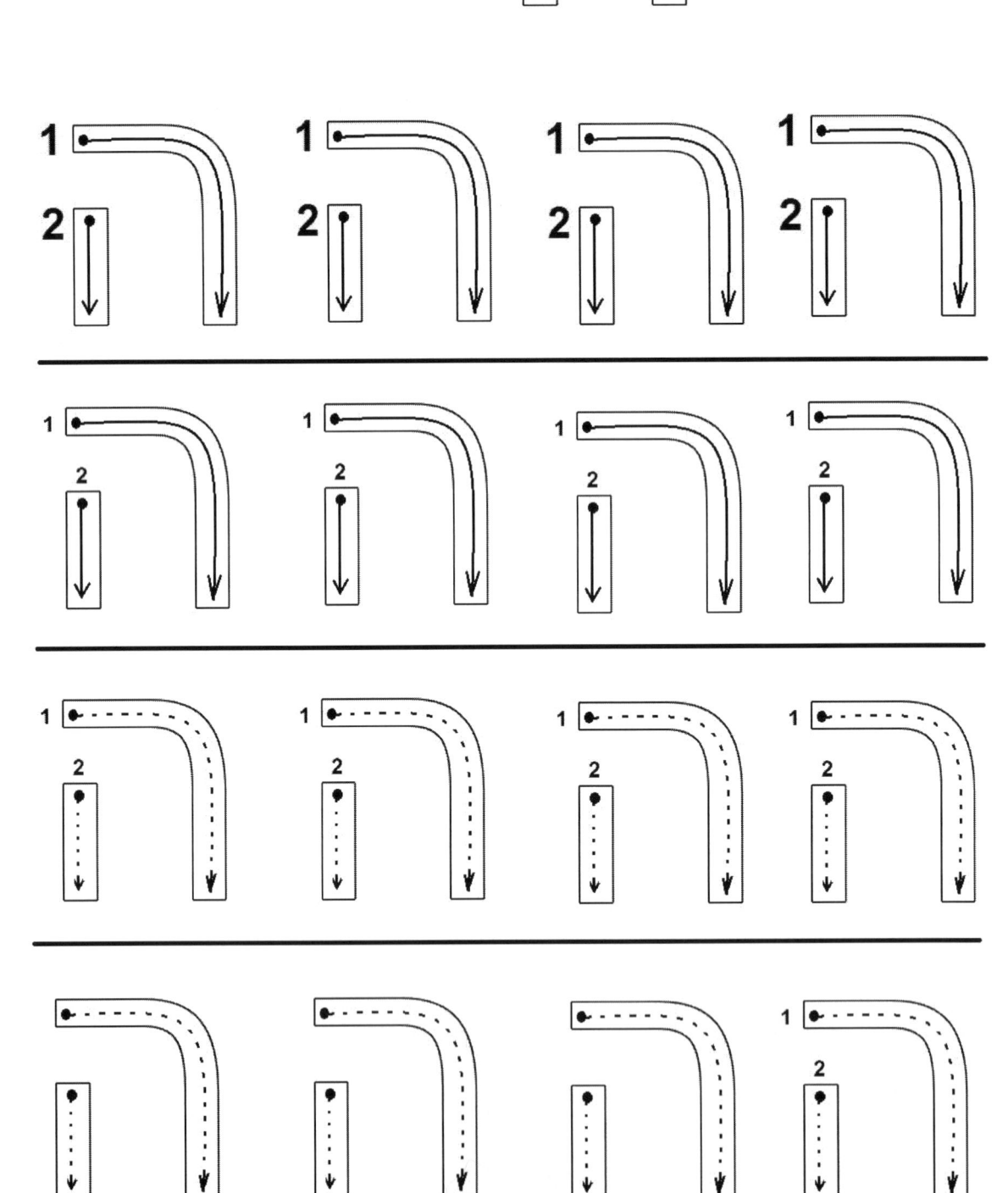

Hey ה

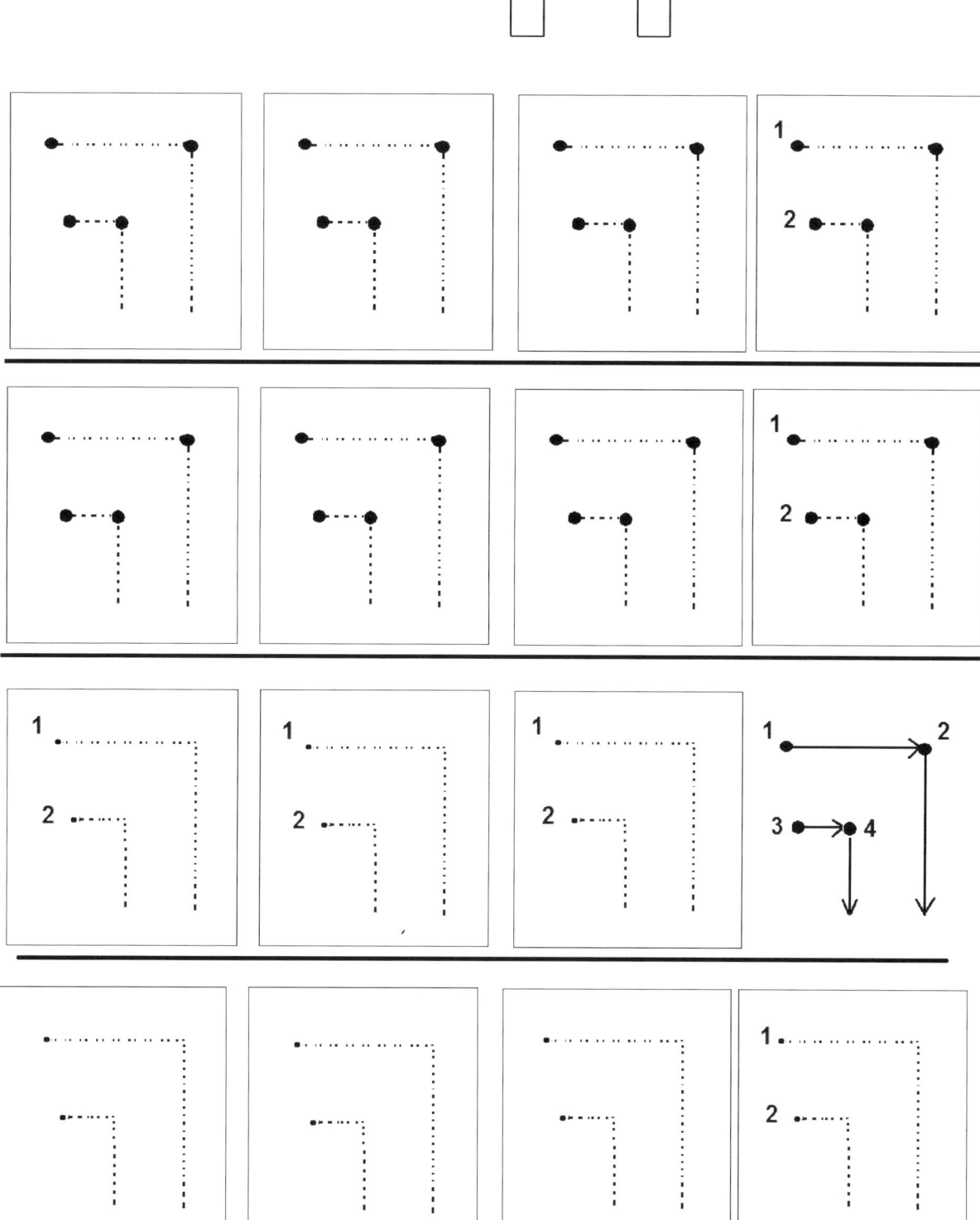

Hey ה

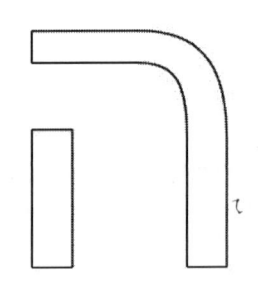

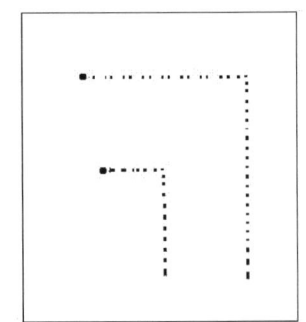

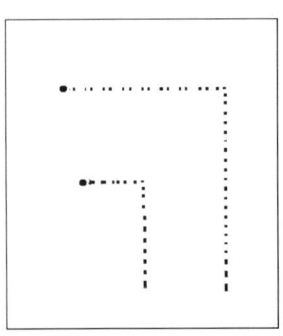

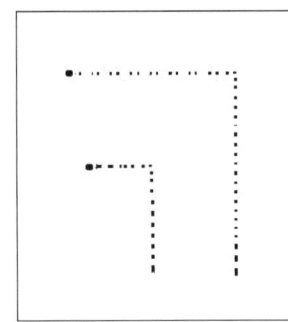

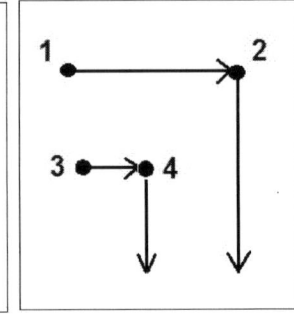

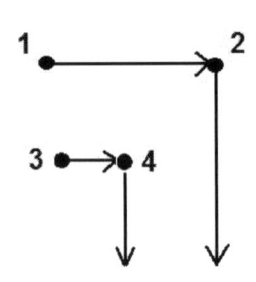

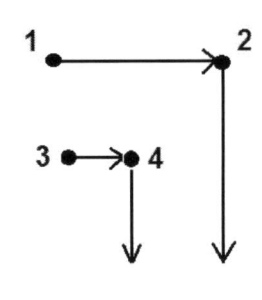

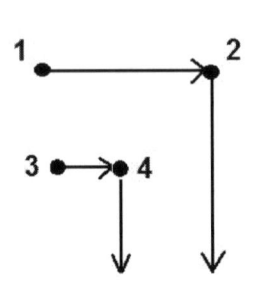

Say the Alef-Bet:

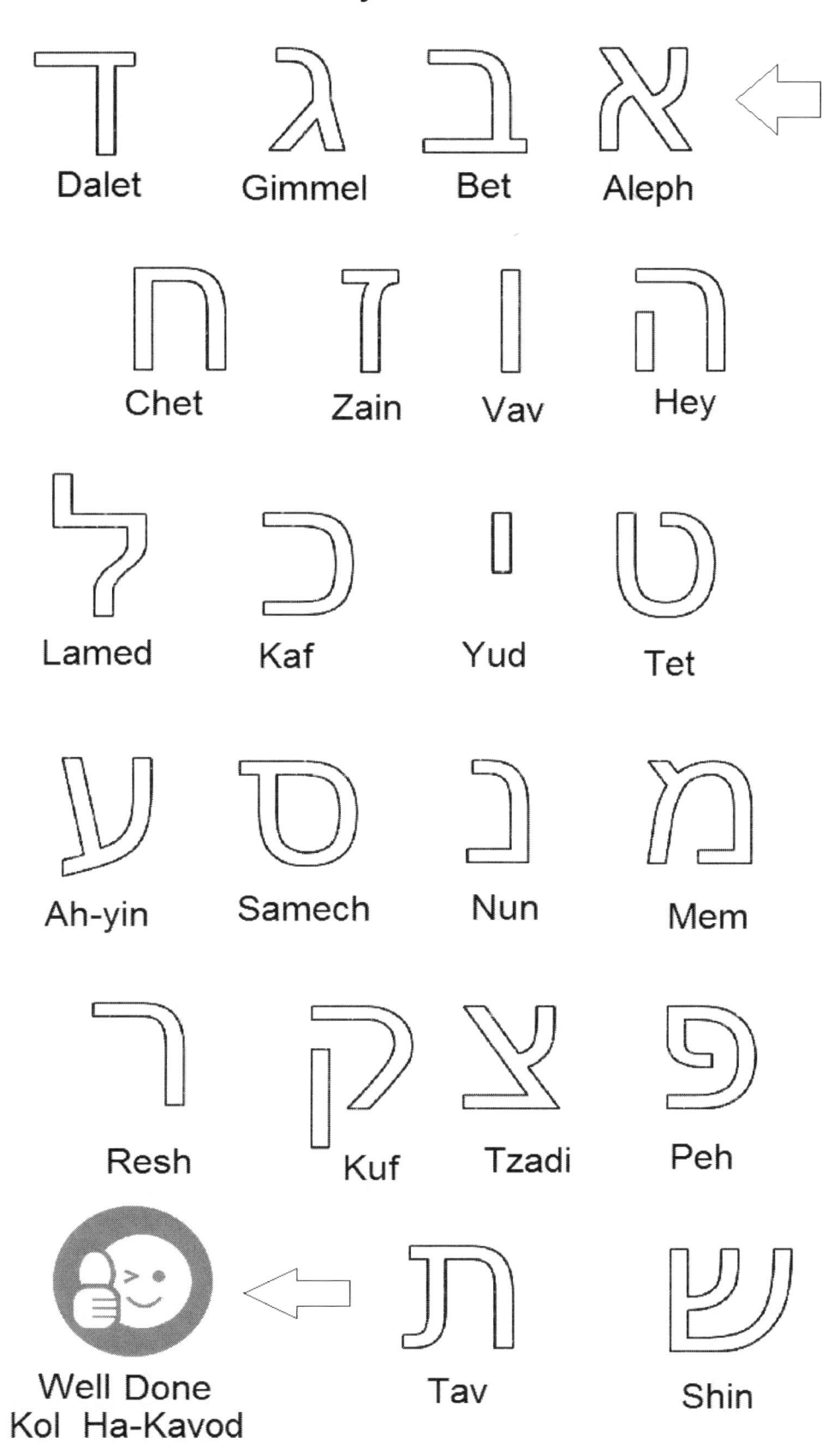

ד ג ב א ←
Dalet Gimmel Bet Aleph

ח ז ו ה
Chet Zain Vav Hey

ל כ י ט
Lamed Kaf Yud Tet

ע ס נ מ
Ah-yin Samech Nun Mem

ר ק צ פ
Resh Kuf Tzadi Peh

← ת ש
Well Done
Kol Ha-Kavod   Tav   Shin

Vav

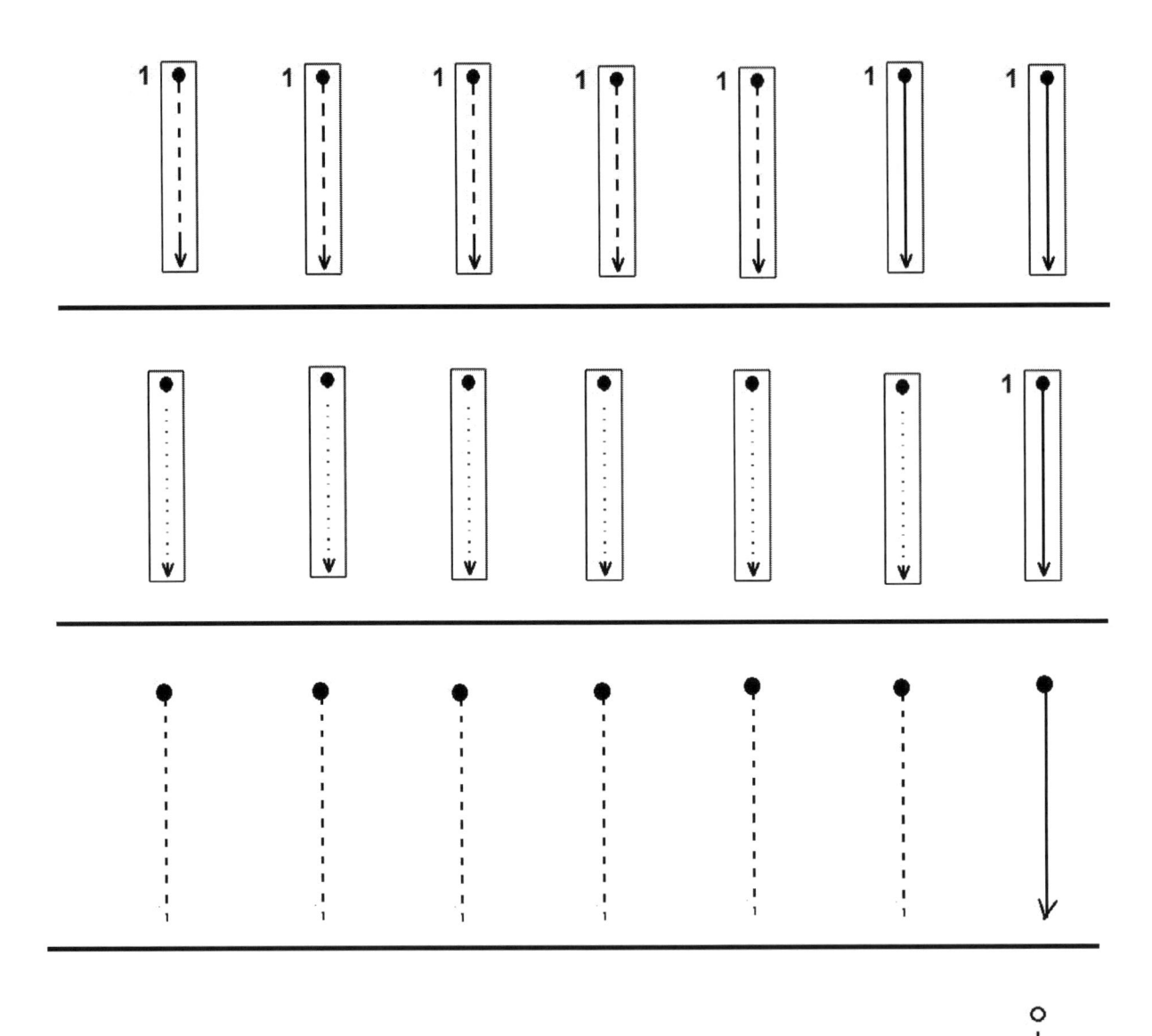

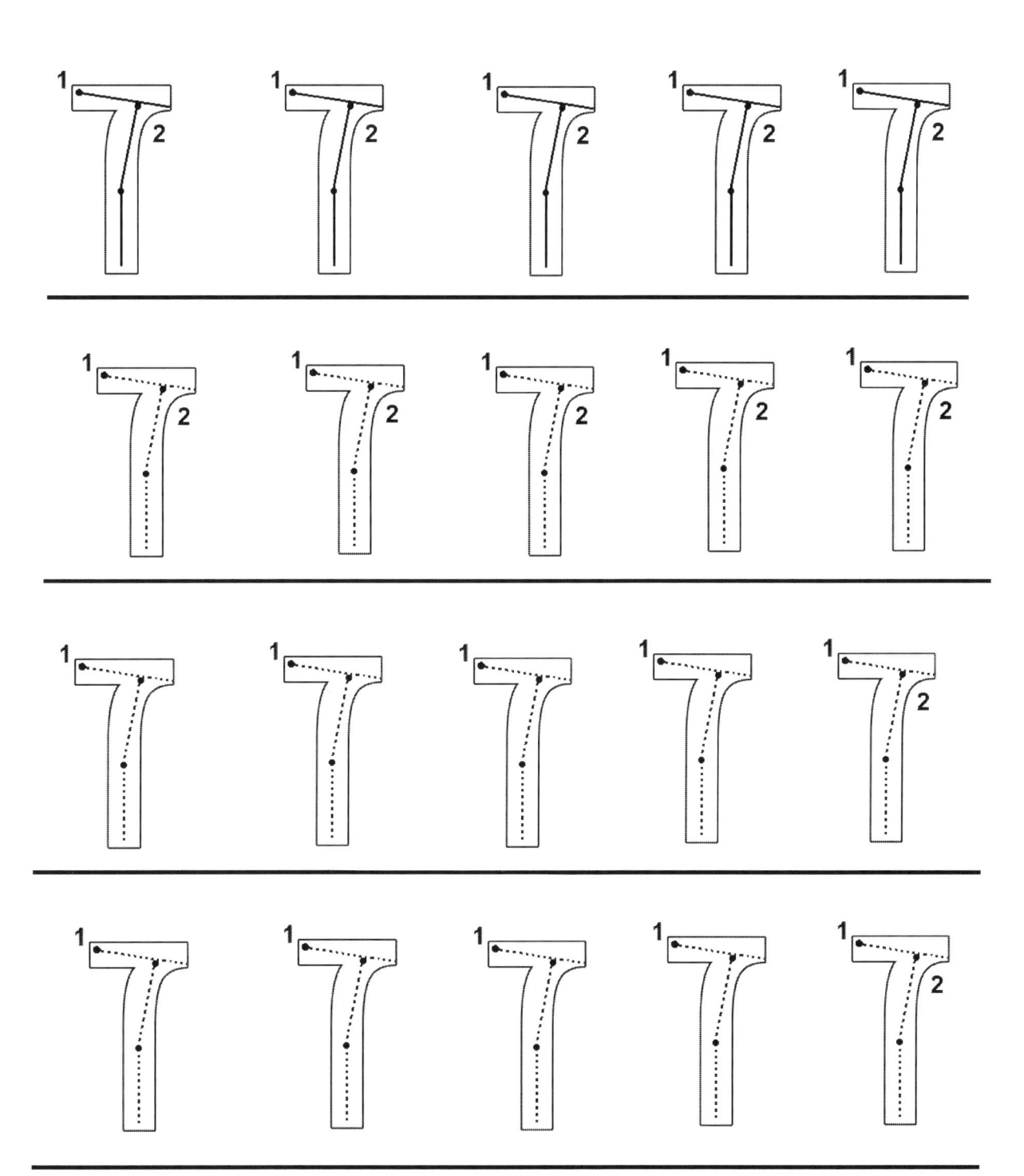

Zain

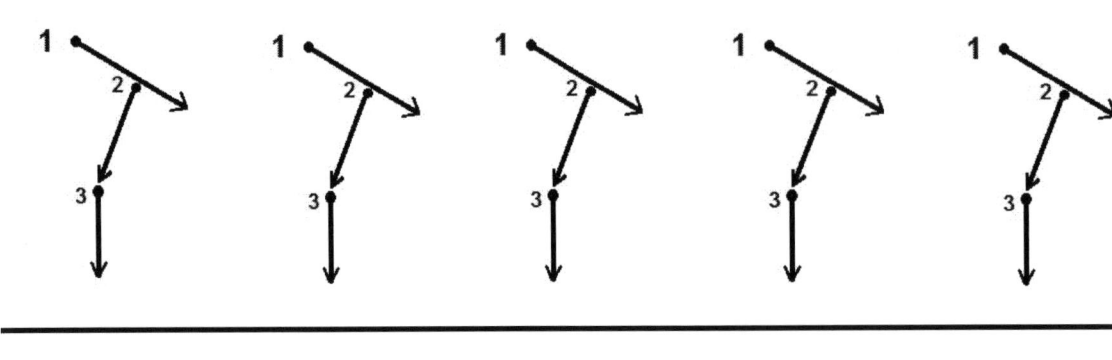

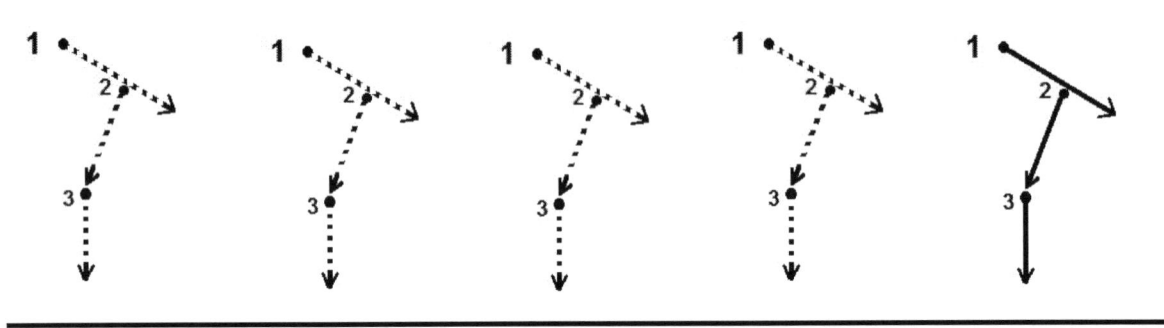

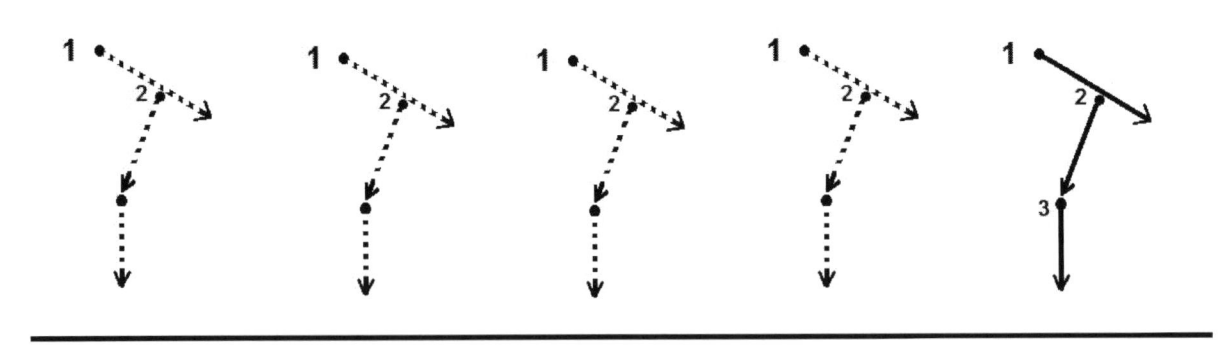

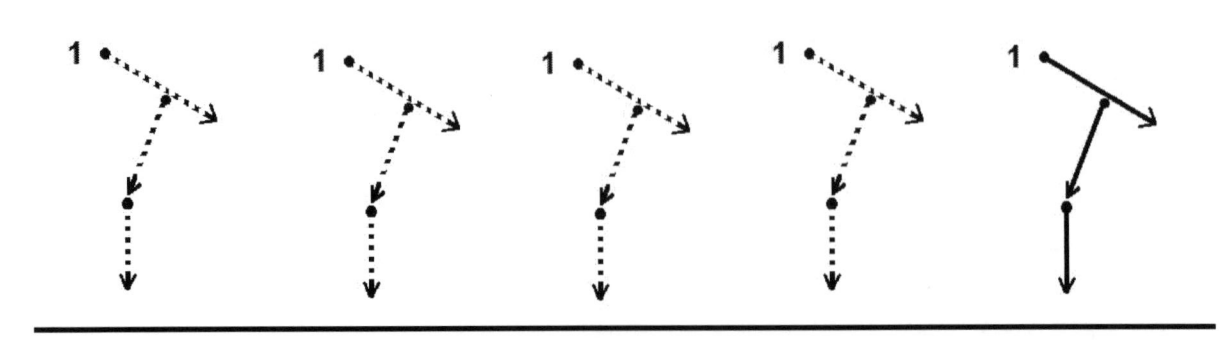

Zain

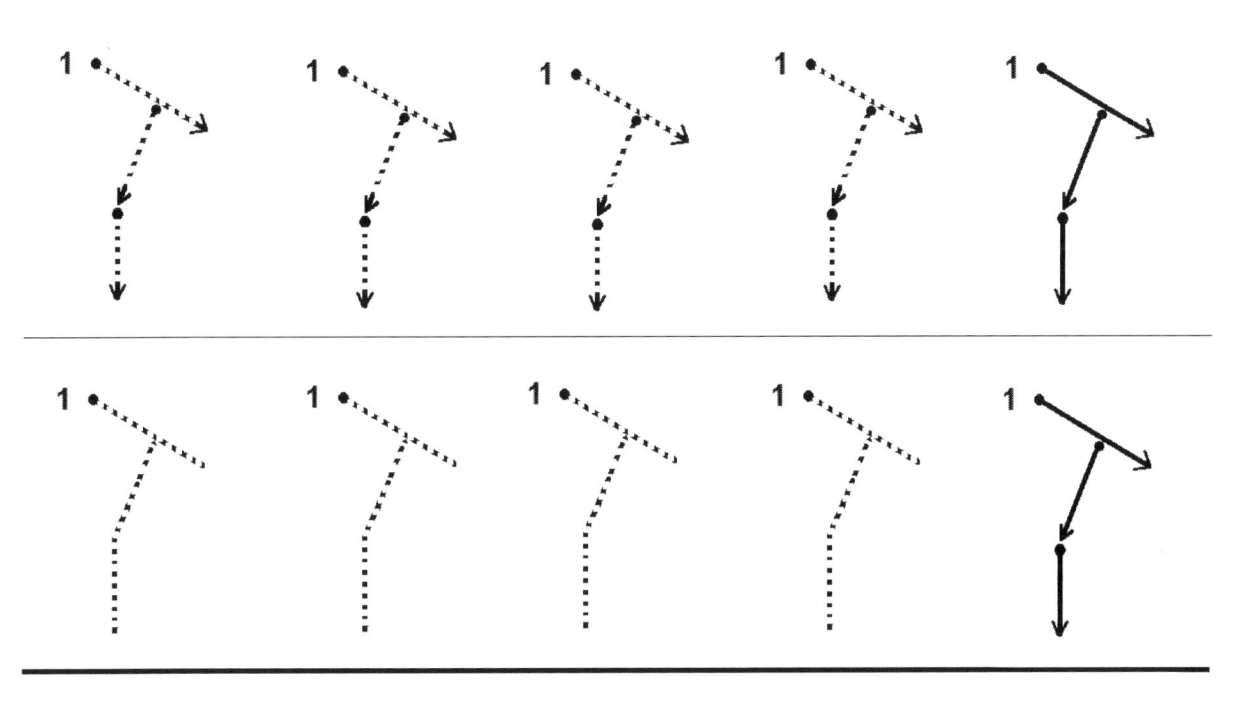

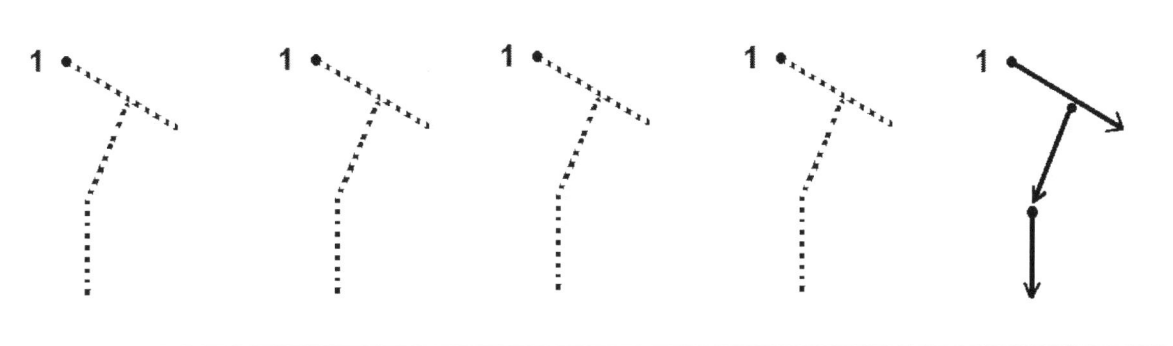

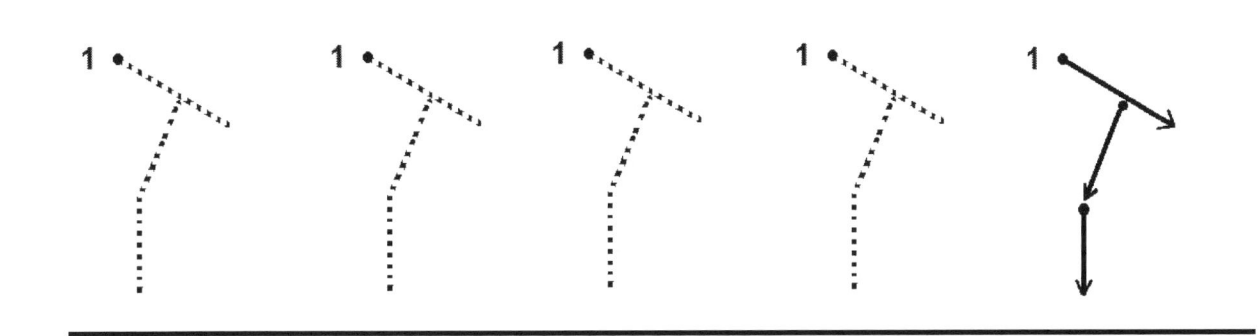

Zain

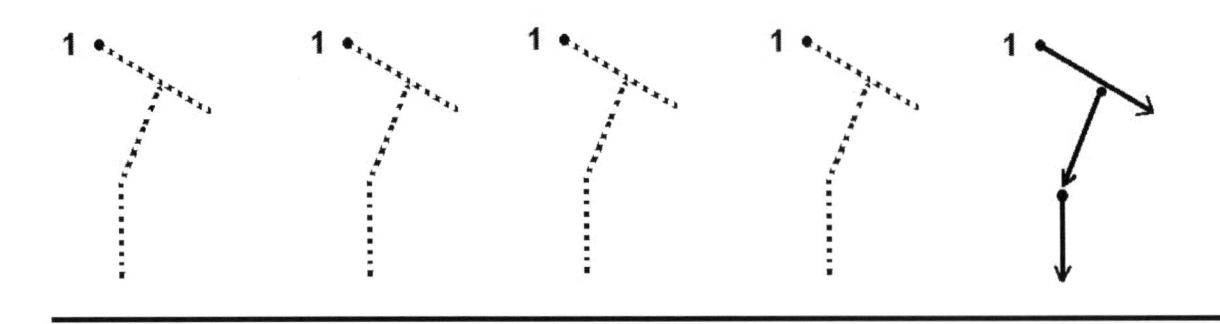

Zain

Chet (Het) ח

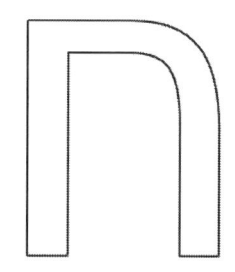

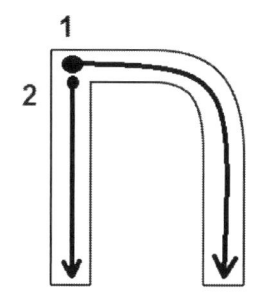

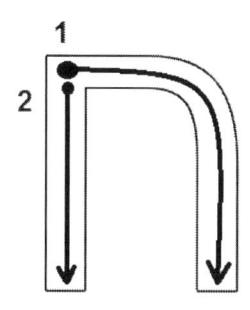

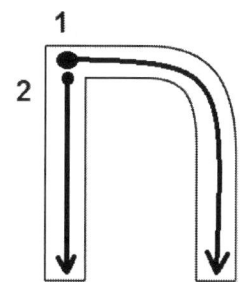

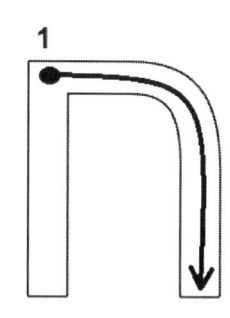

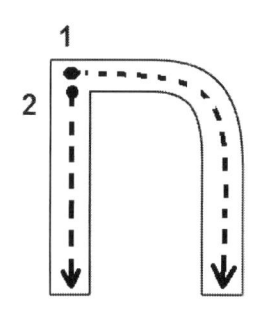

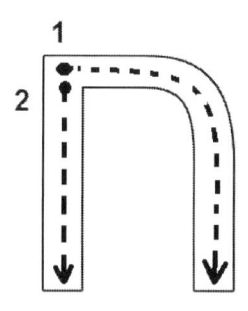

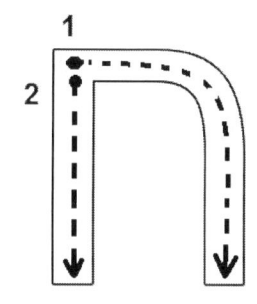

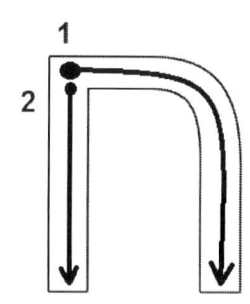

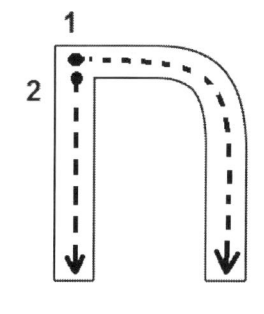

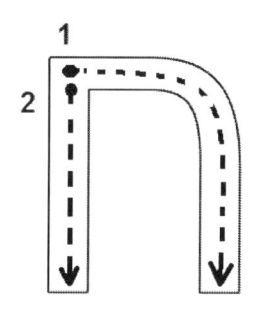

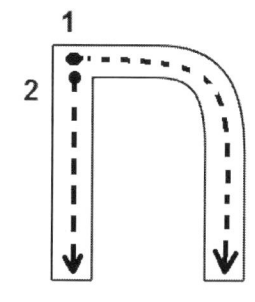

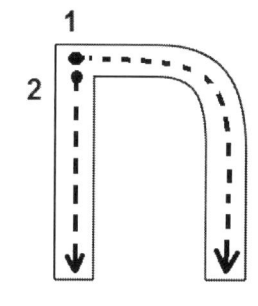

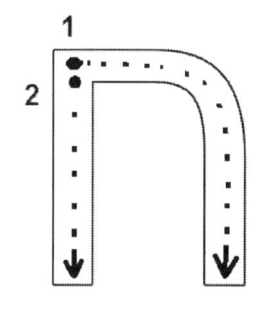

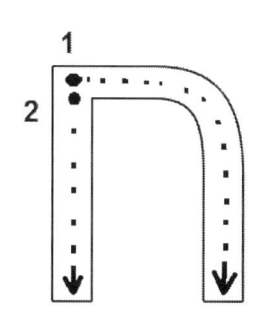

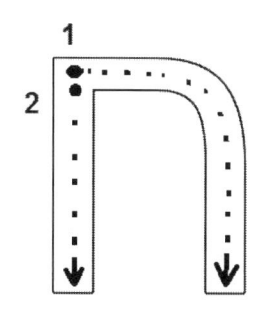

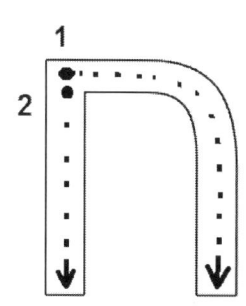

Chet (Het)

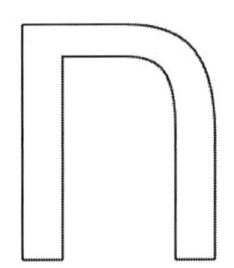

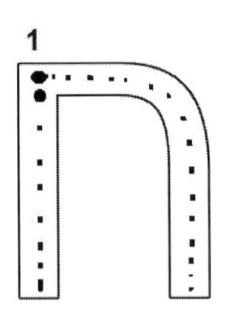

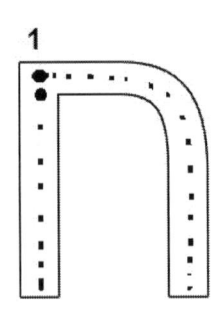

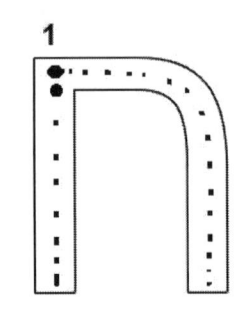

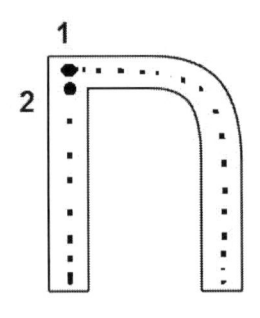

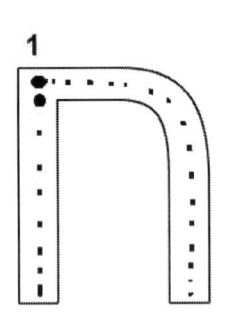

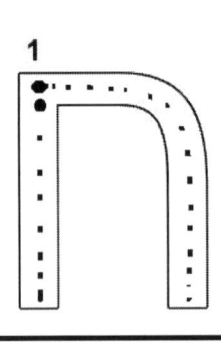

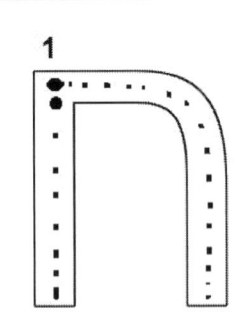

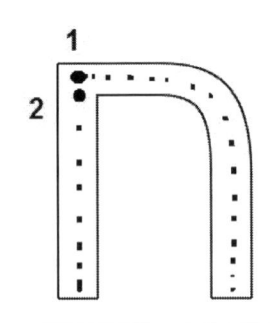

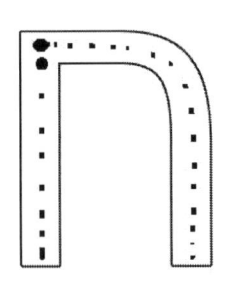

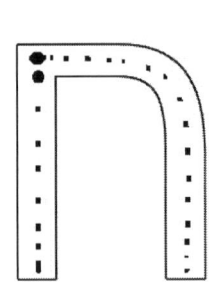

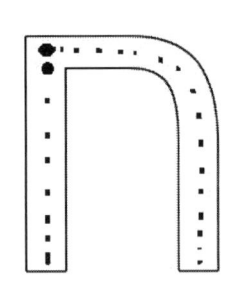

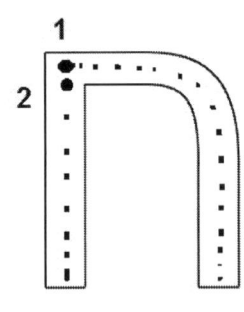

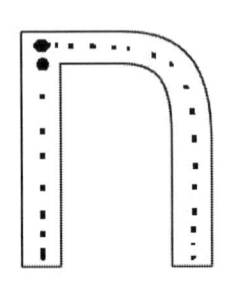

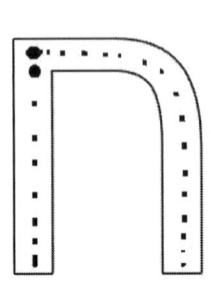

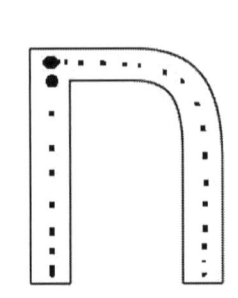

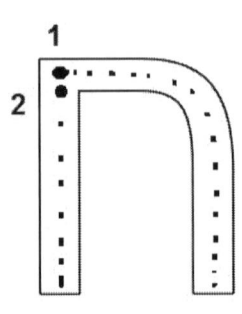

Chet (Het) ח

Chet (Het)

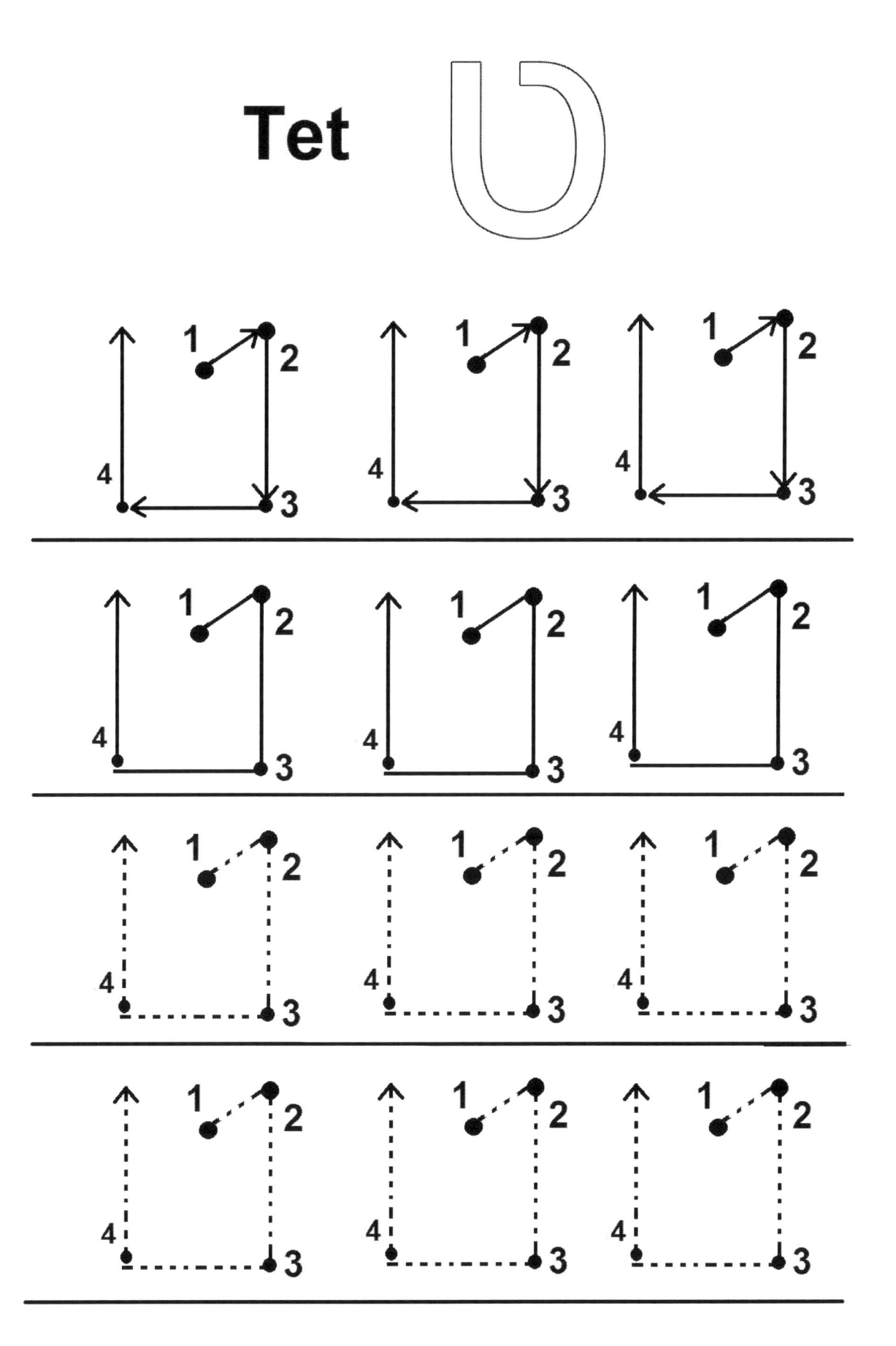

Tet

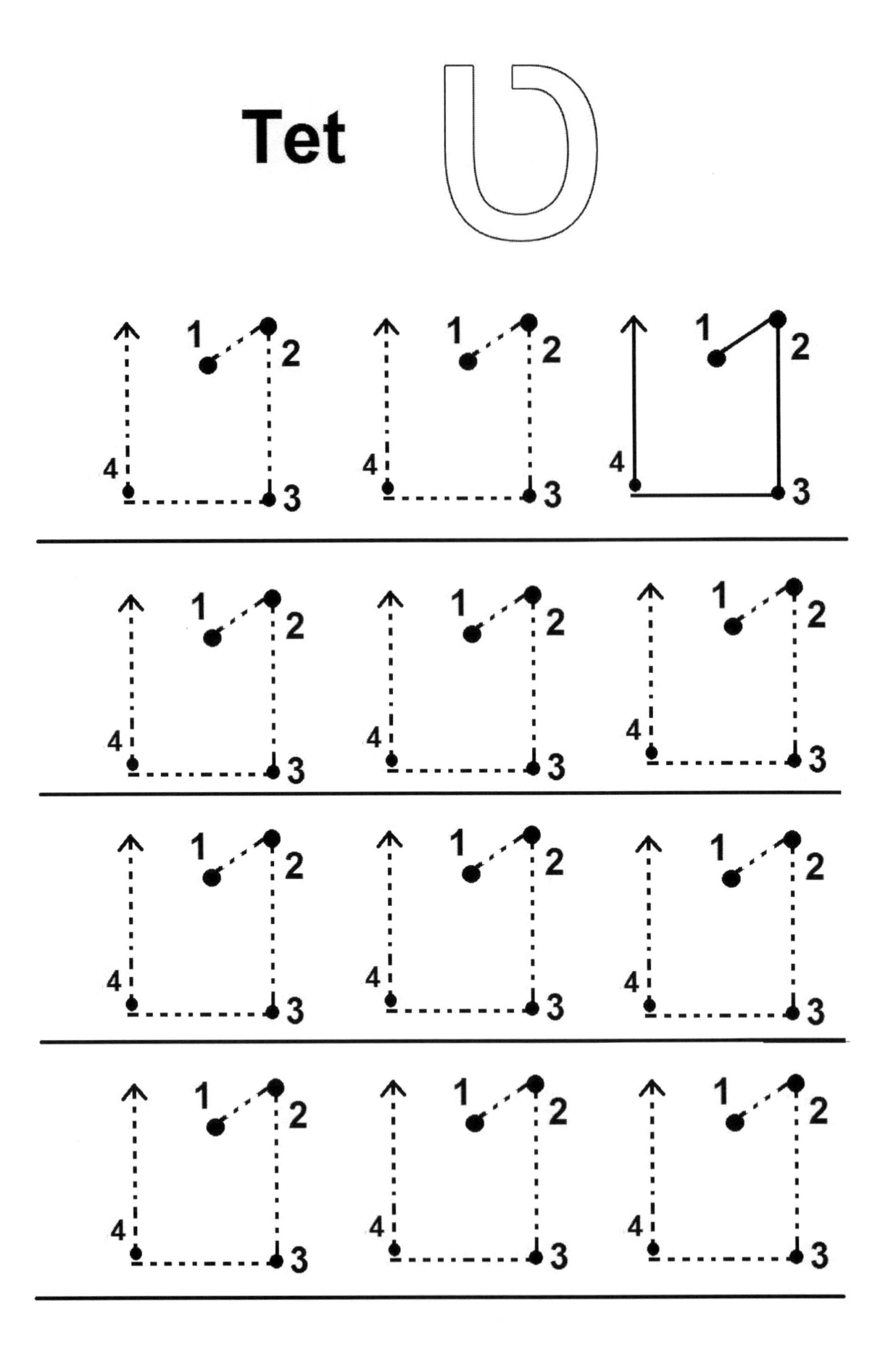

Tet

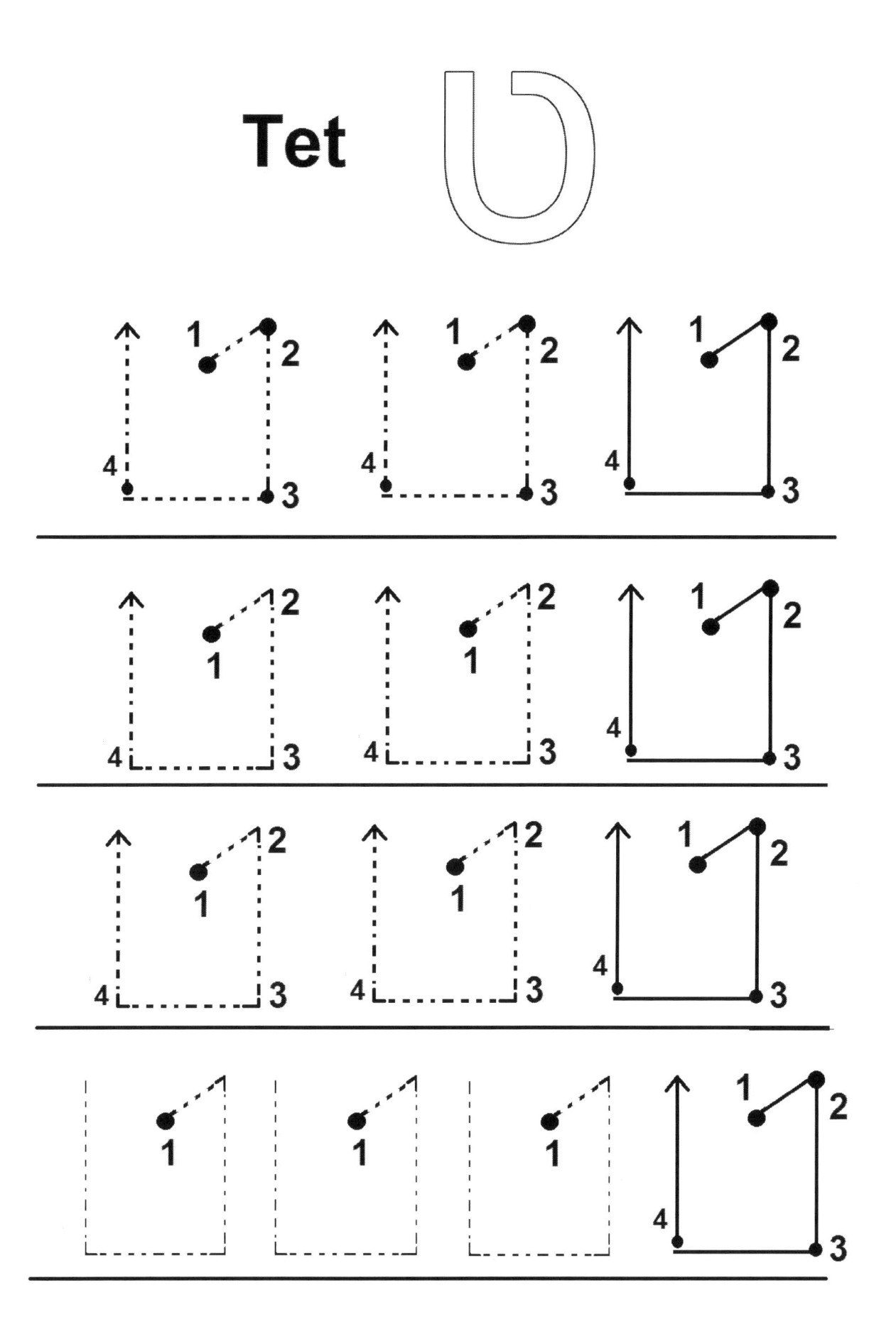

Tet

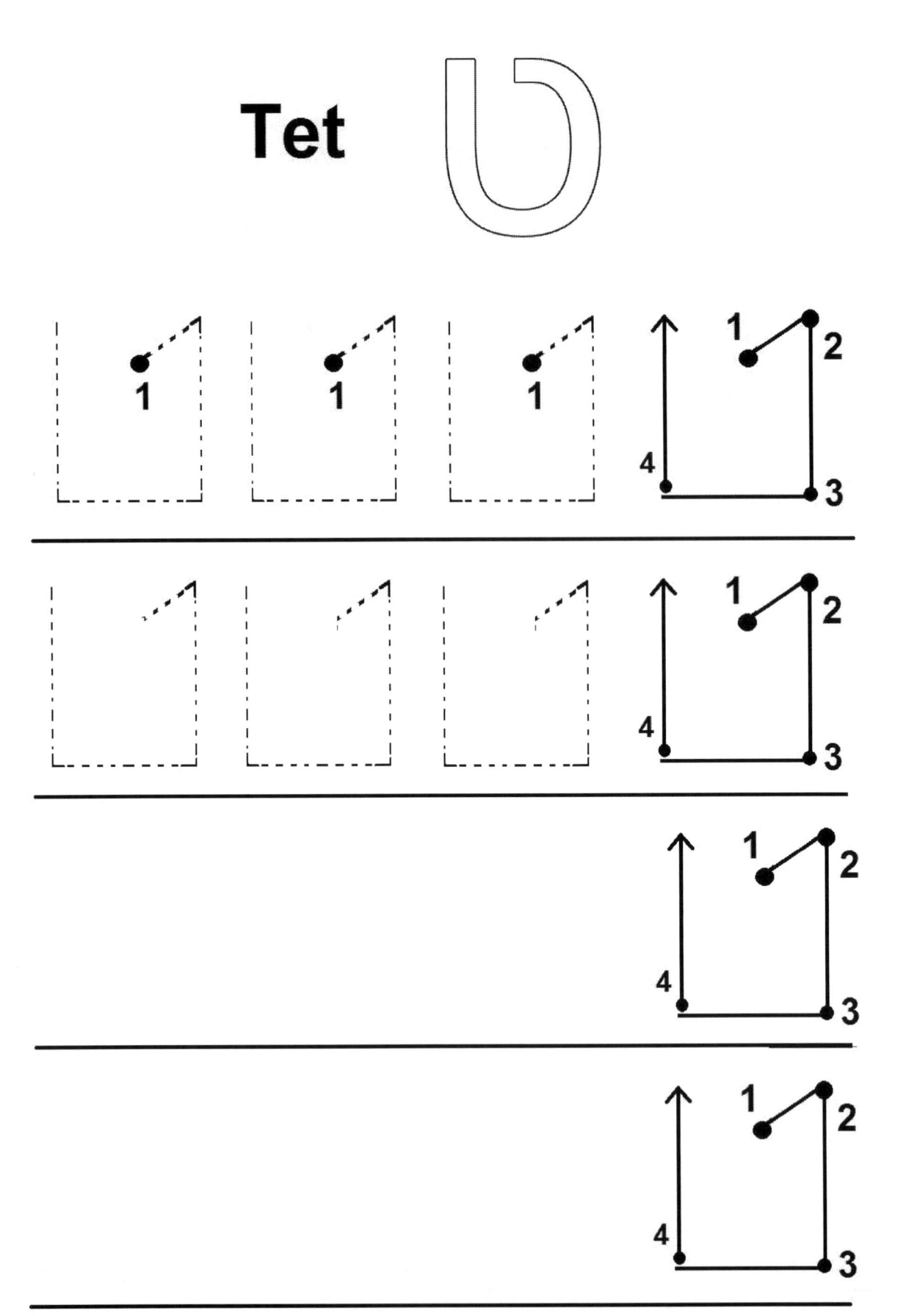

Tet

36

Notice the Yud position is above the line.

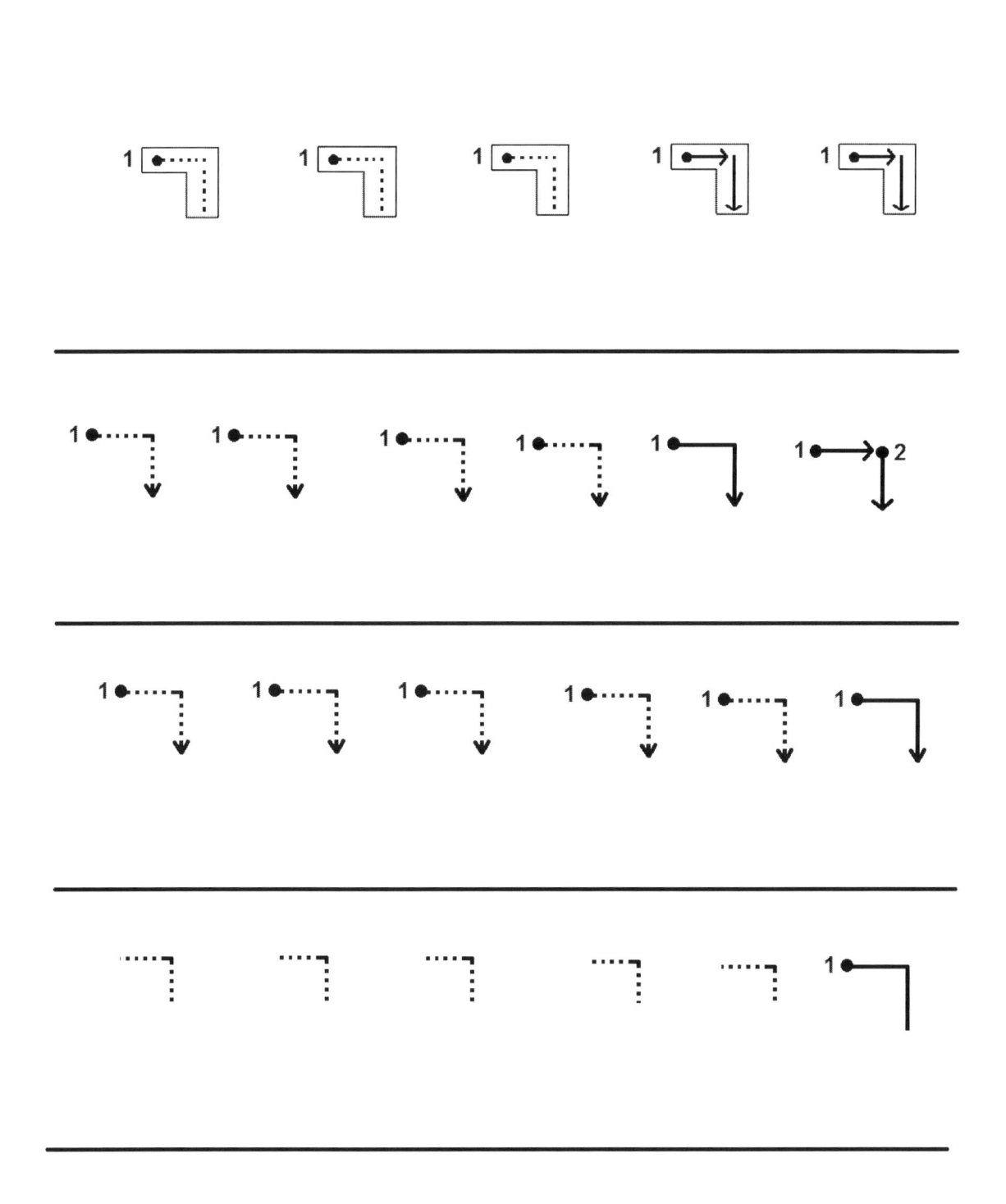

Yud

Yud

The Yud Position

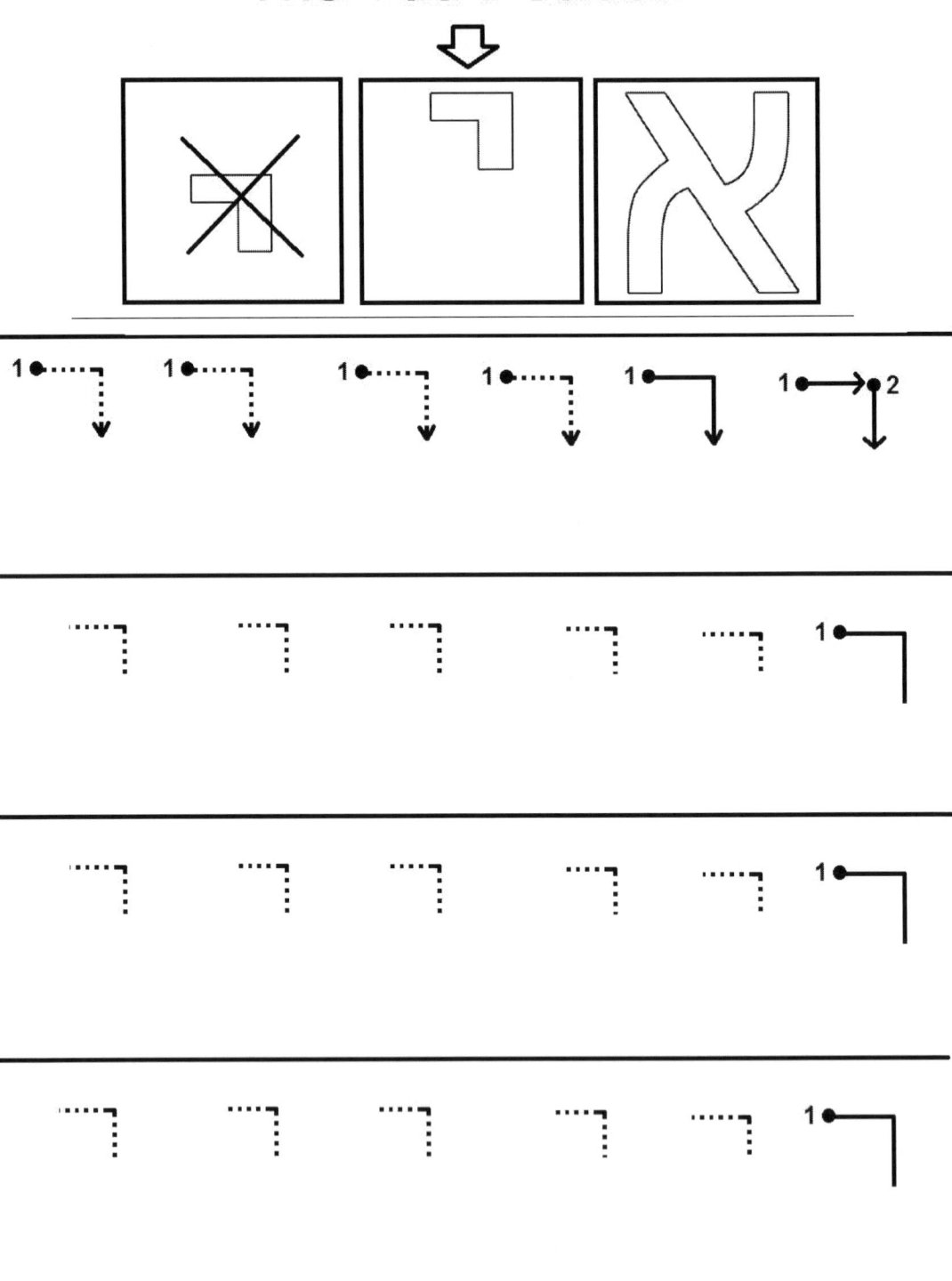

Connect the letter to its name

Tet · Zain · Hey · Yud · Alef · Gimmel · Bet · Dalet · Vav · Chet

Practice Writing The Hebrew Letters

Alef א

Bet ב

Gimel ג

Dalet ד

Hey ה

Vav ו

Zain ז

Chet ח

Tet ט

Yud י

Say the Alef-bet

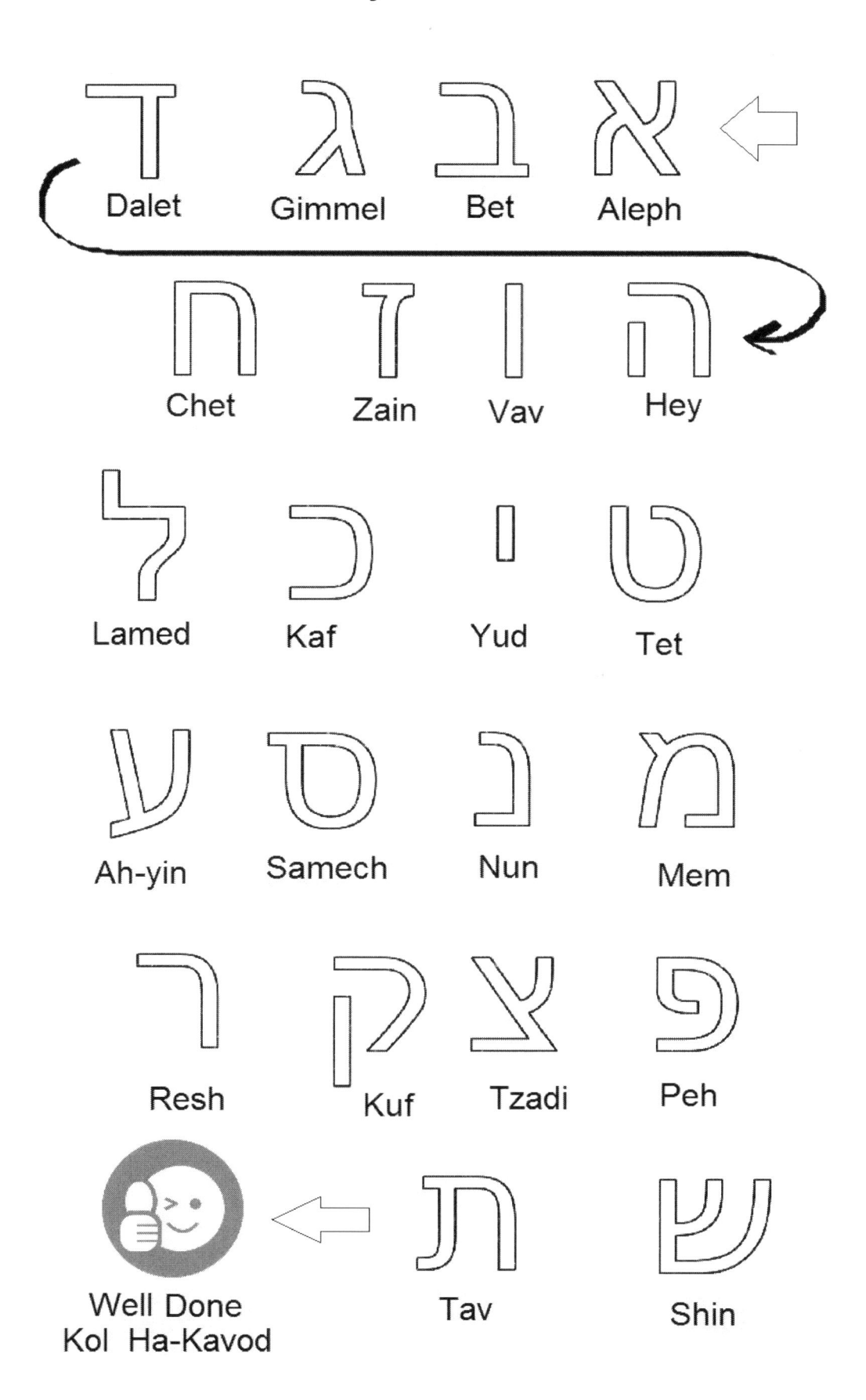

ד	ג	ב	א
Dalet	Gimmel	Bet	Aleph

ח	ז	ו	ה
Chet	Zain	Vav	Hey

ל	כ	י	ט
Lamed	Kaf	Yud	Tet

ע	ס	נ	מ
Ah-yin	Samech	Nun	Mem

ר	ק	צ	פ
Resh	Kuf	Tzadi	Peh

ת	ש
Tav	Shin

Well Done
Kol Ha-Kavod

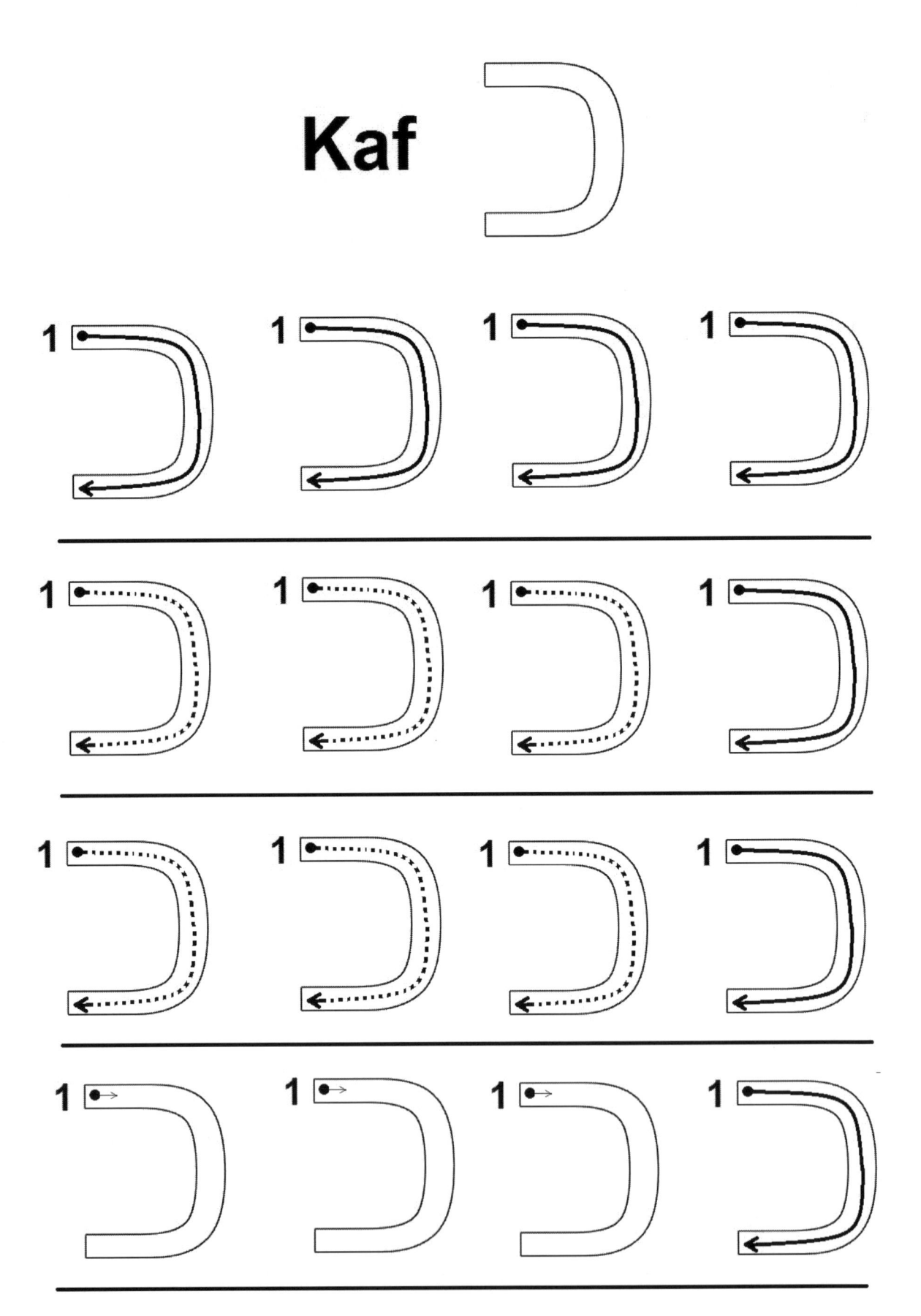

Kaf

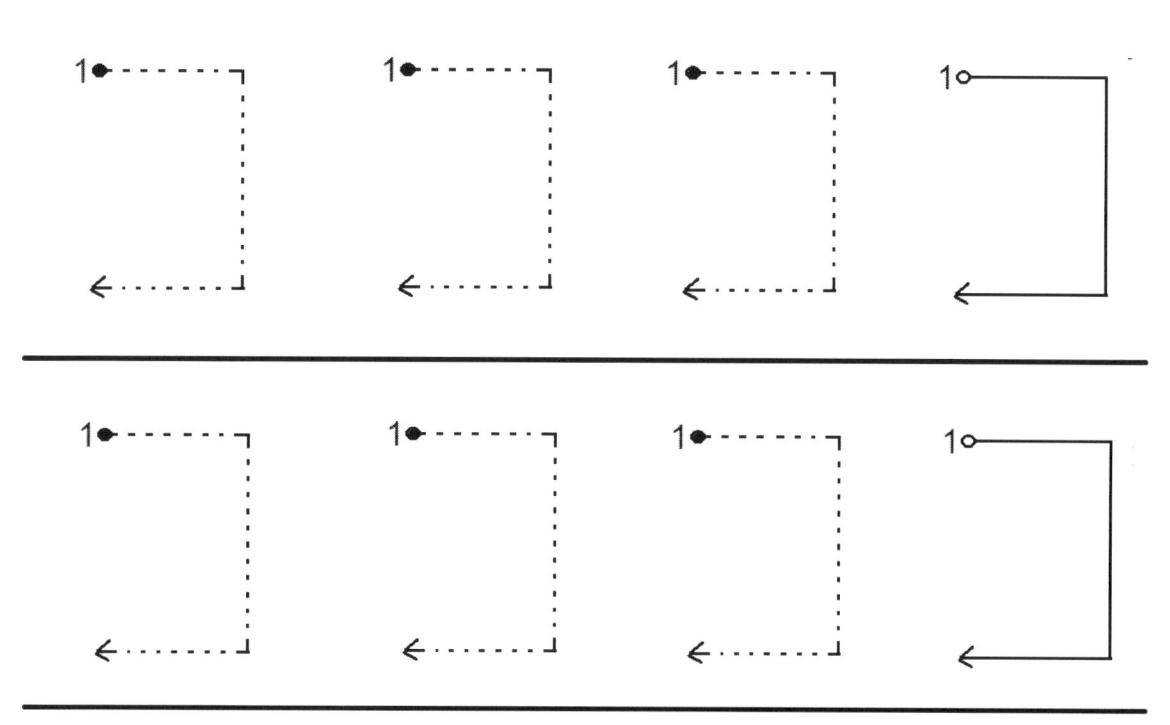

Kaf

Kaf כ

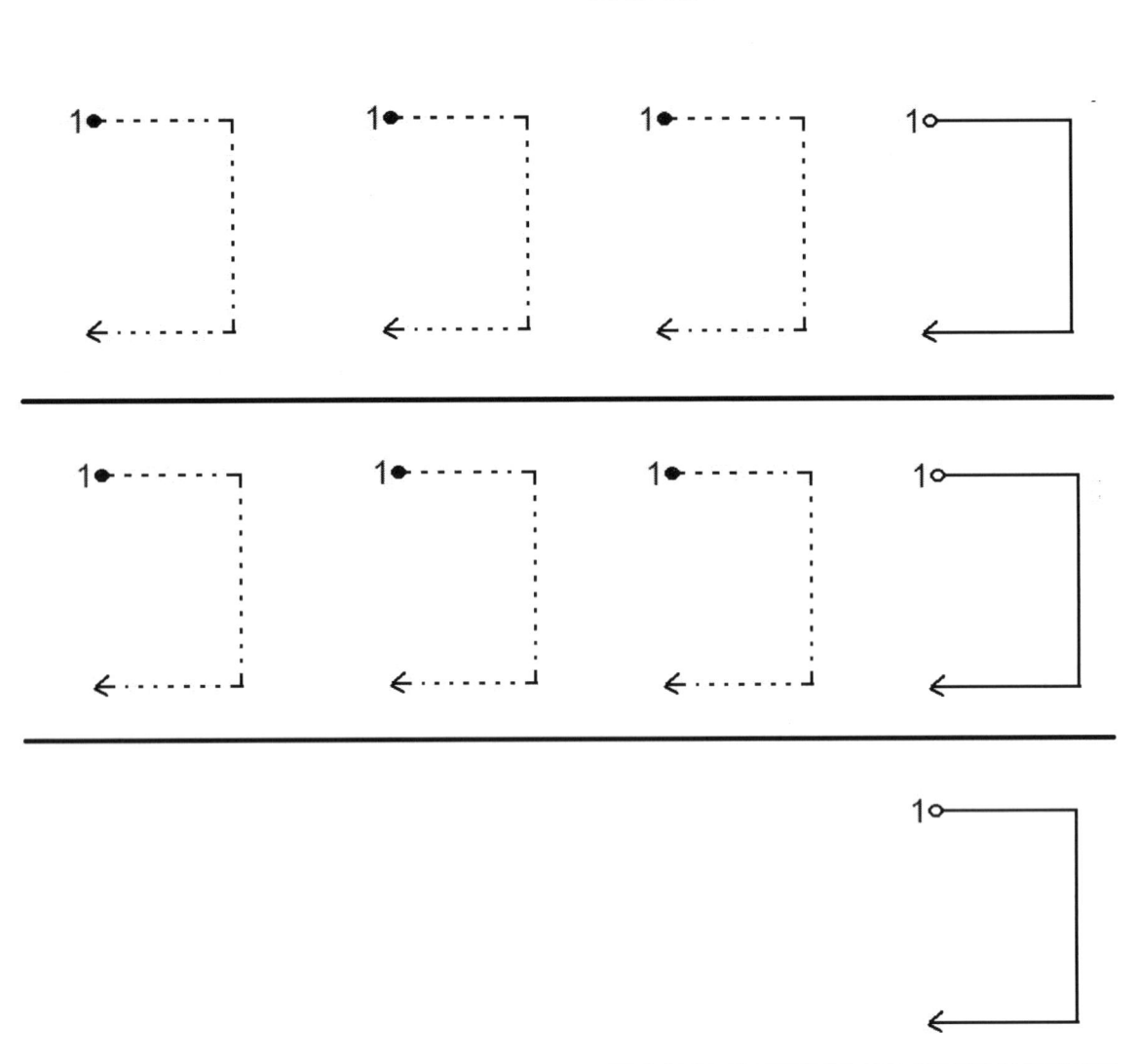

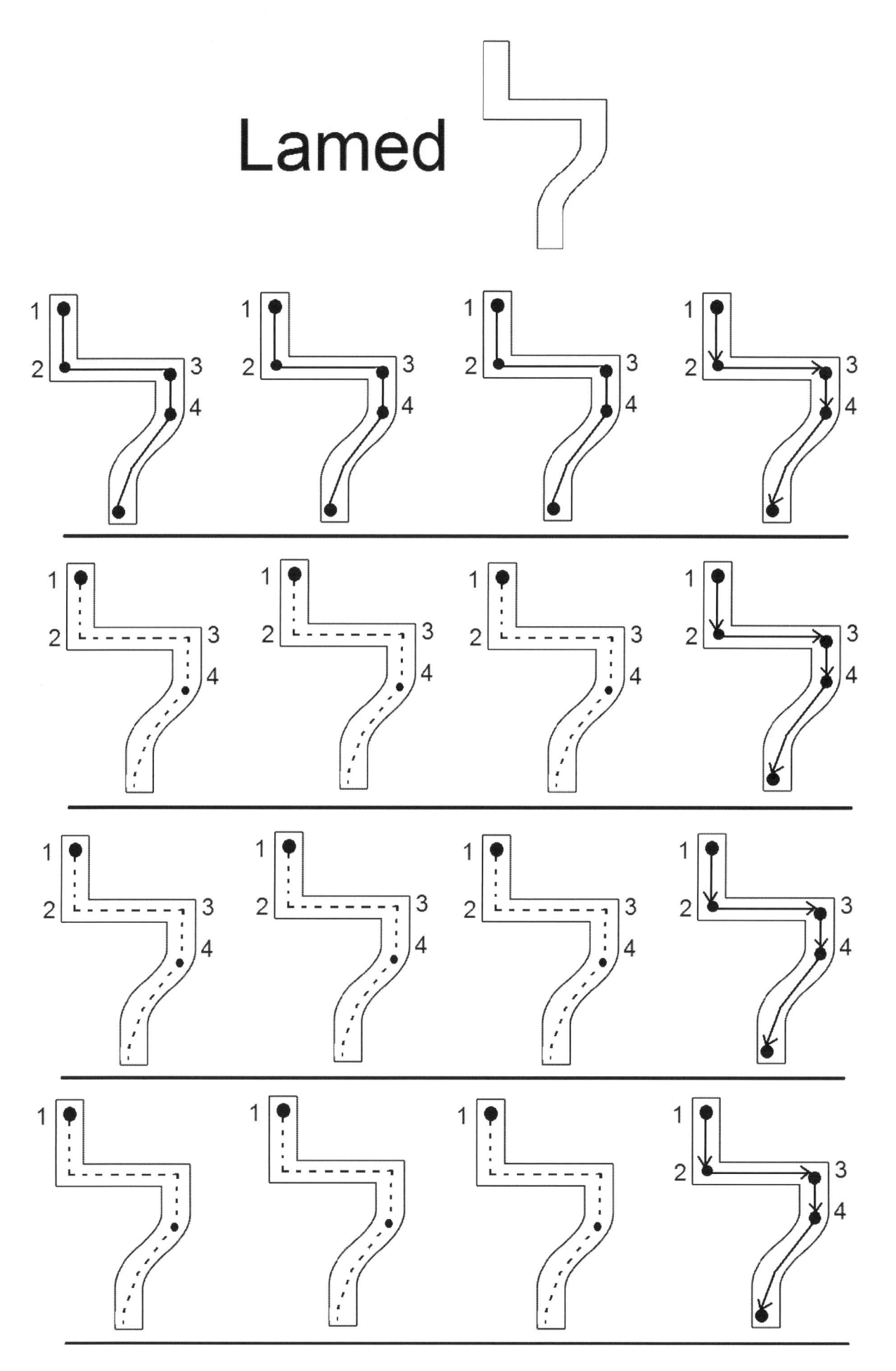

Lamed

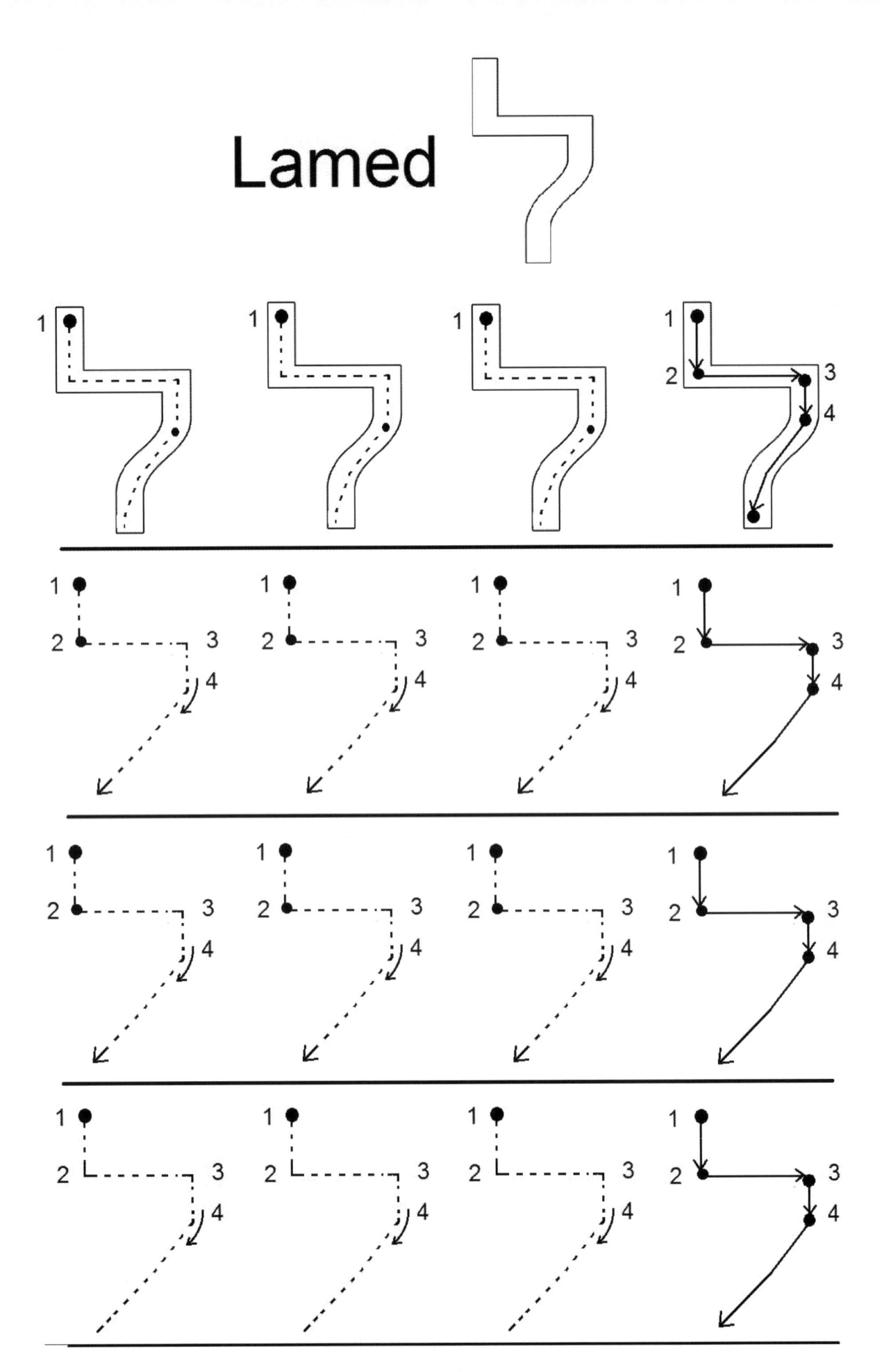

Lamed

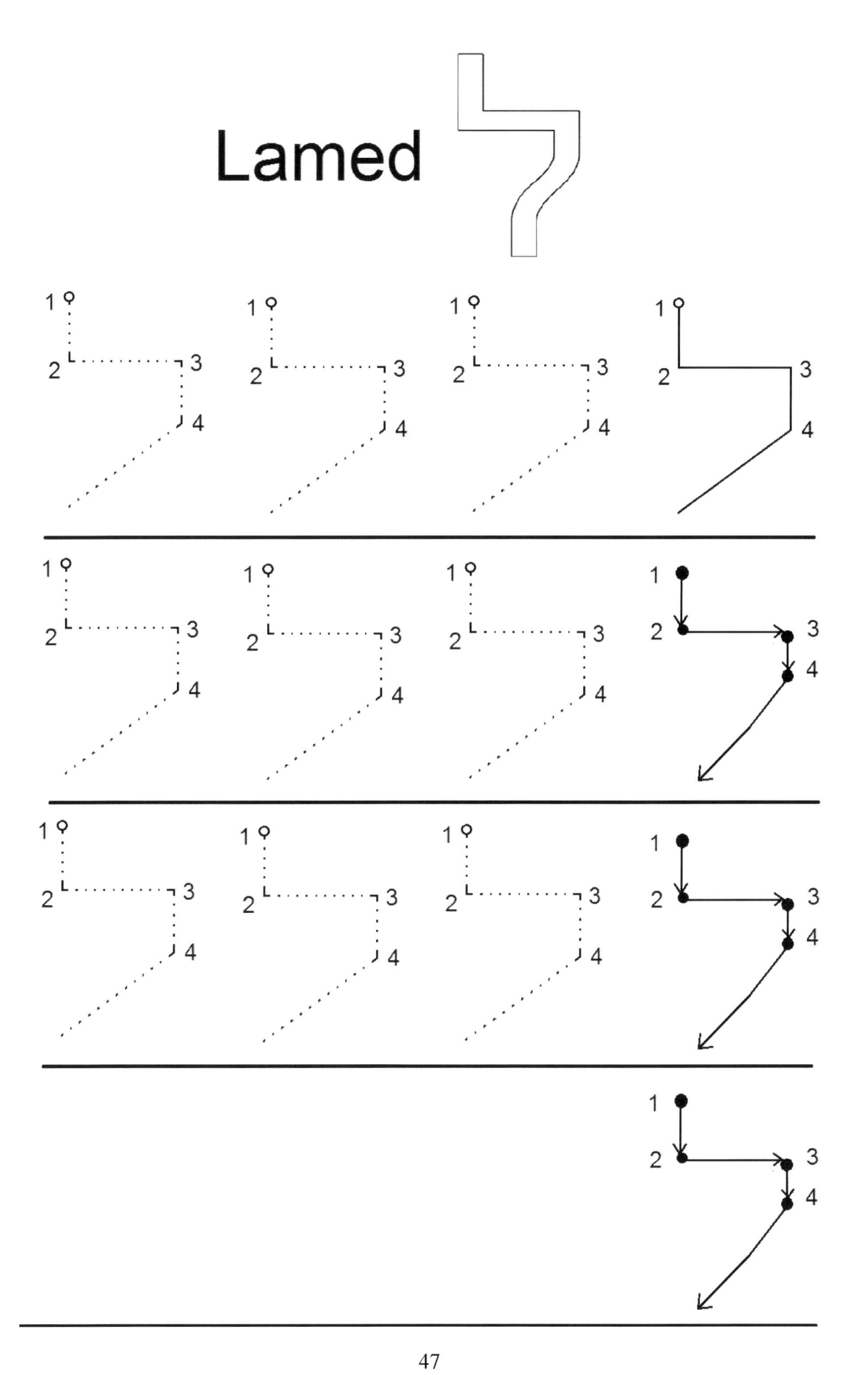

Lamed

Mem מ

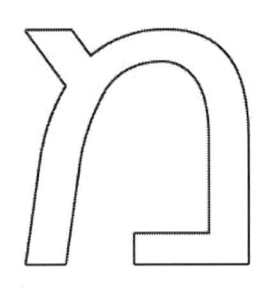

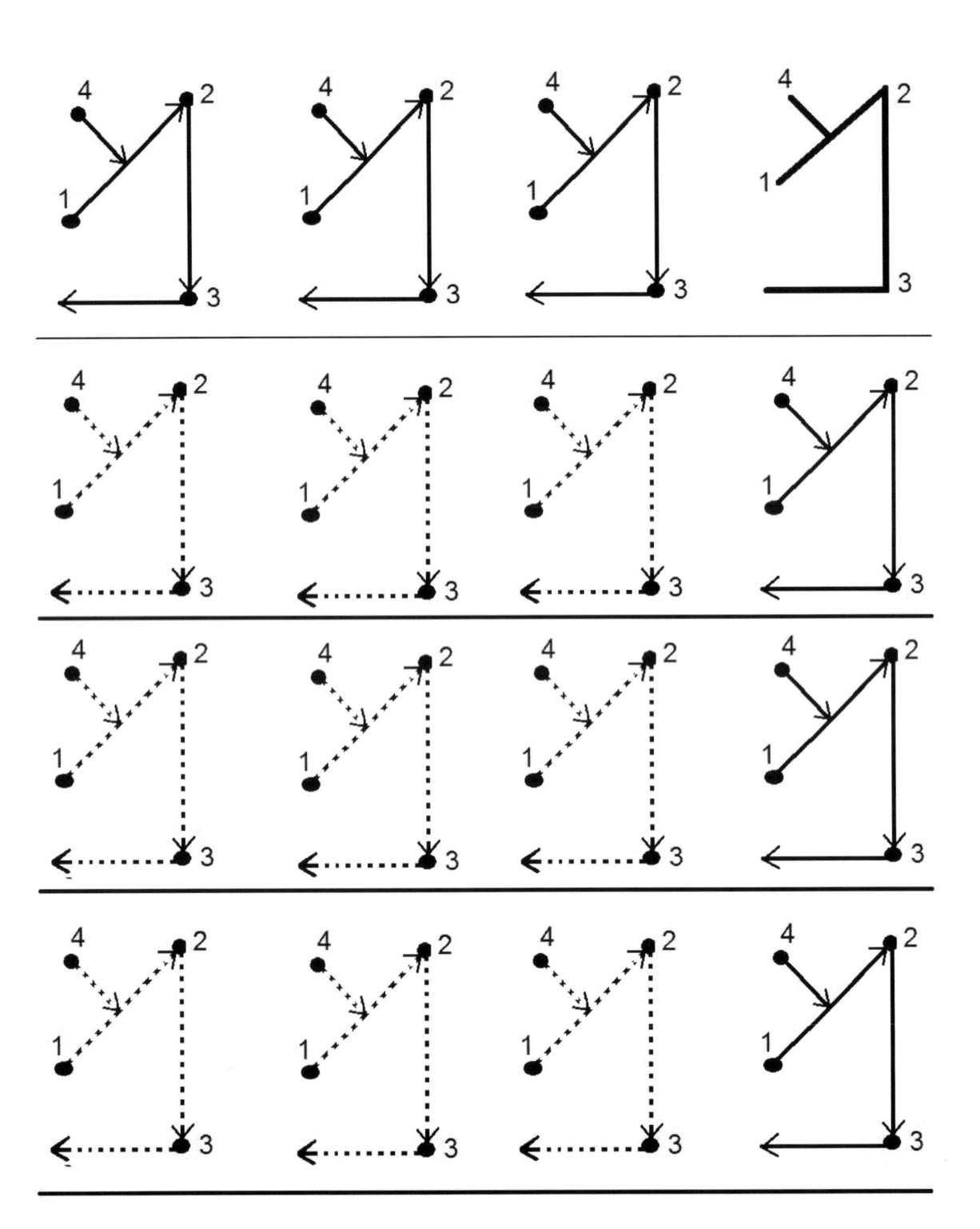

Mem ת

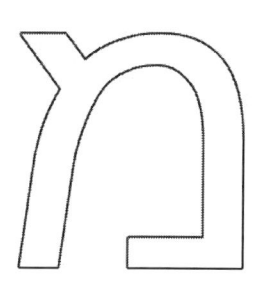

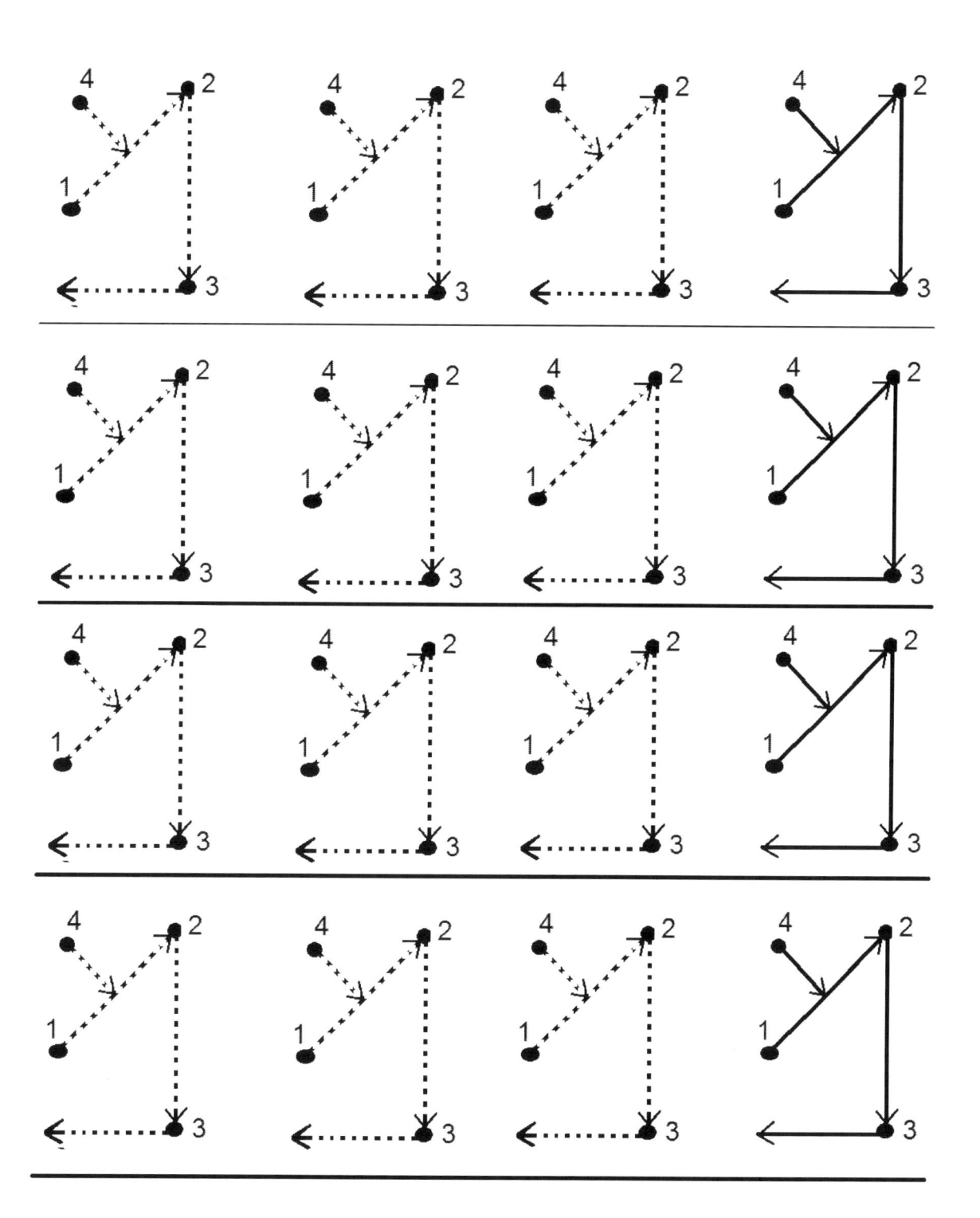

Mem ת

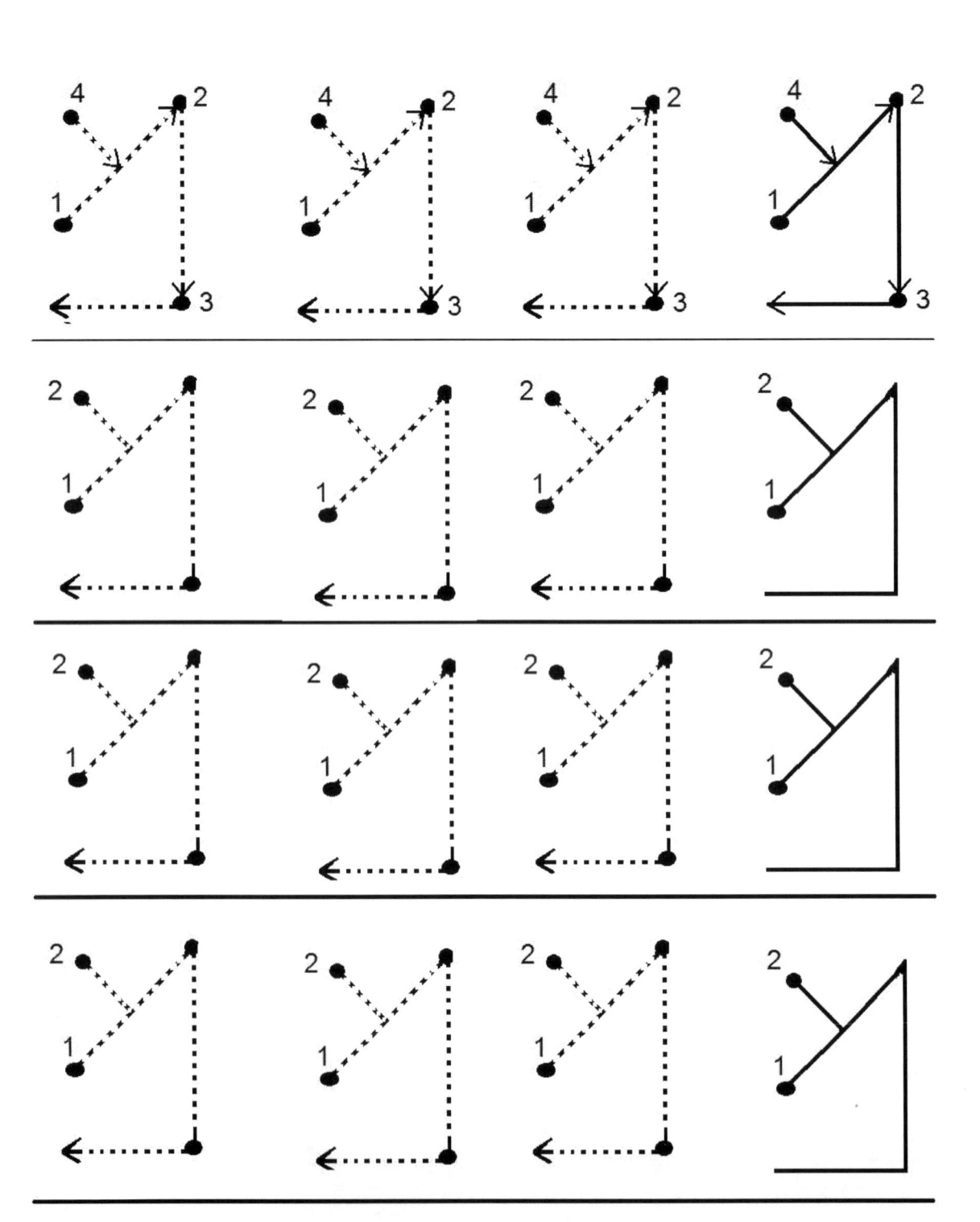

Mem מ

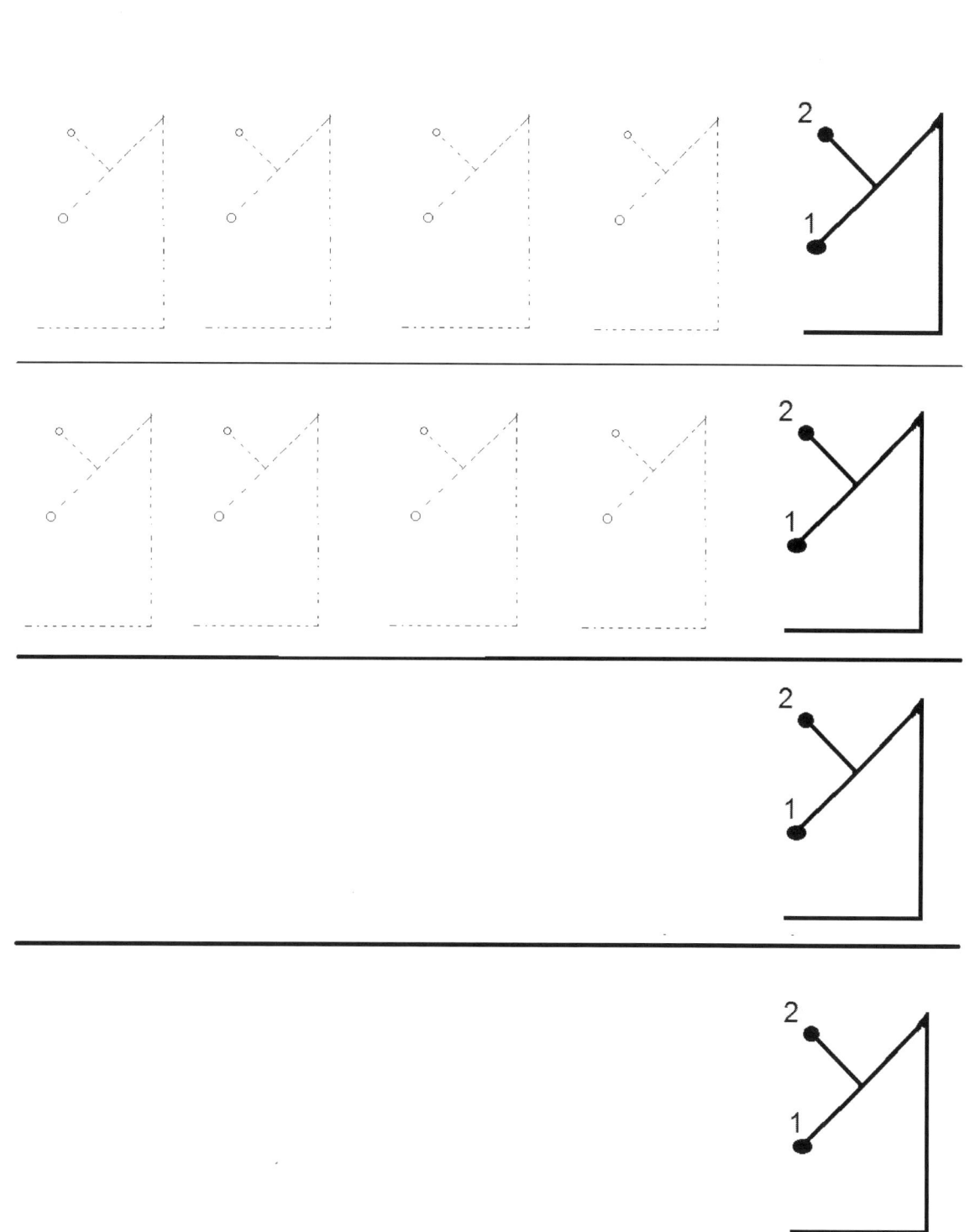

Nun ב

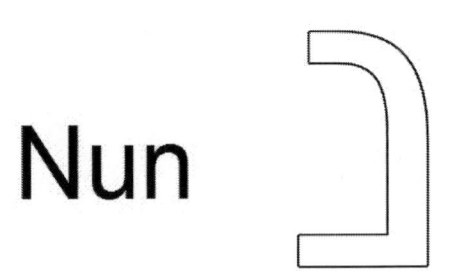

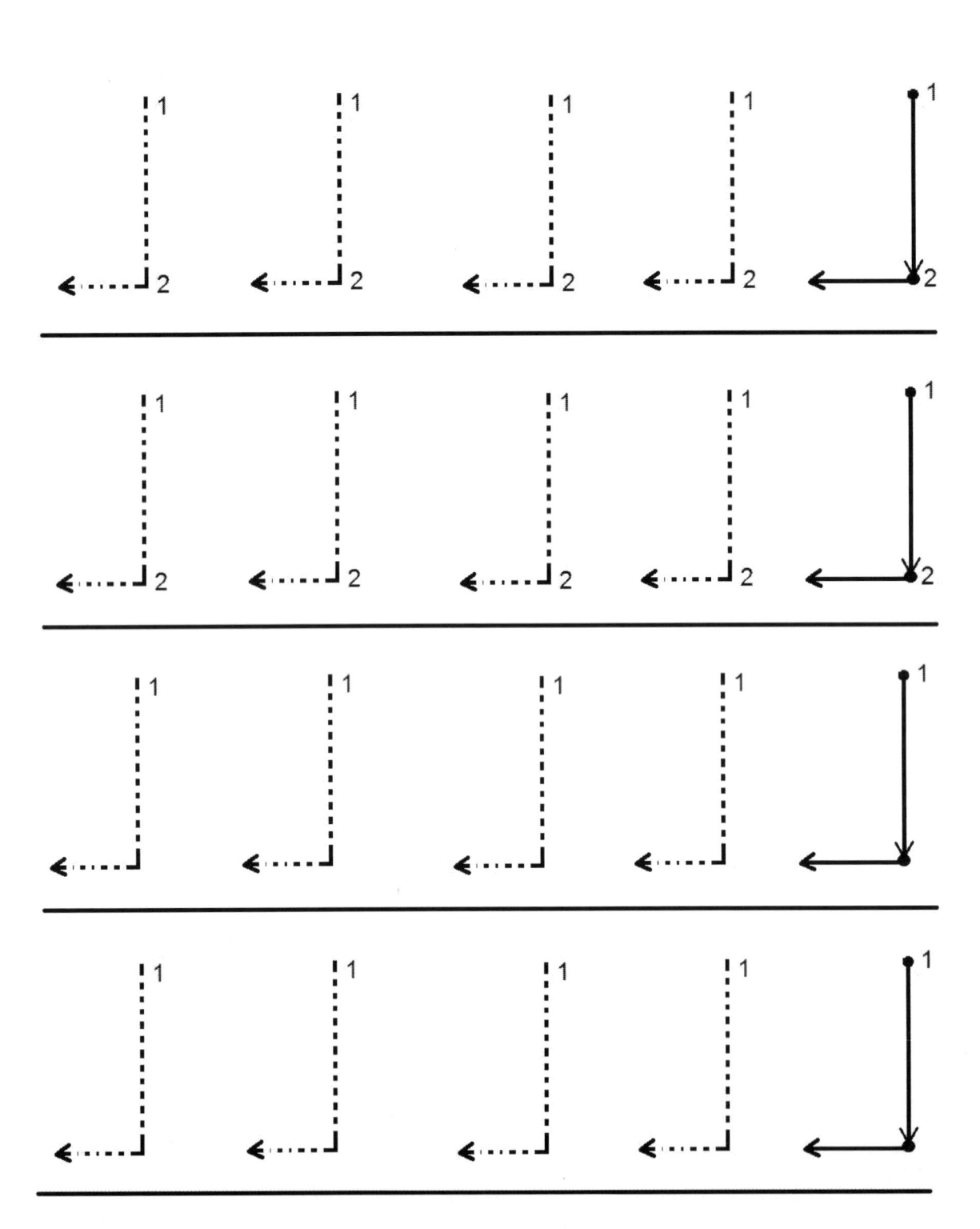

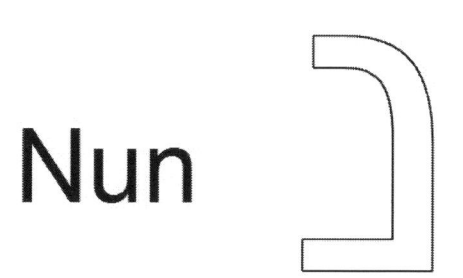

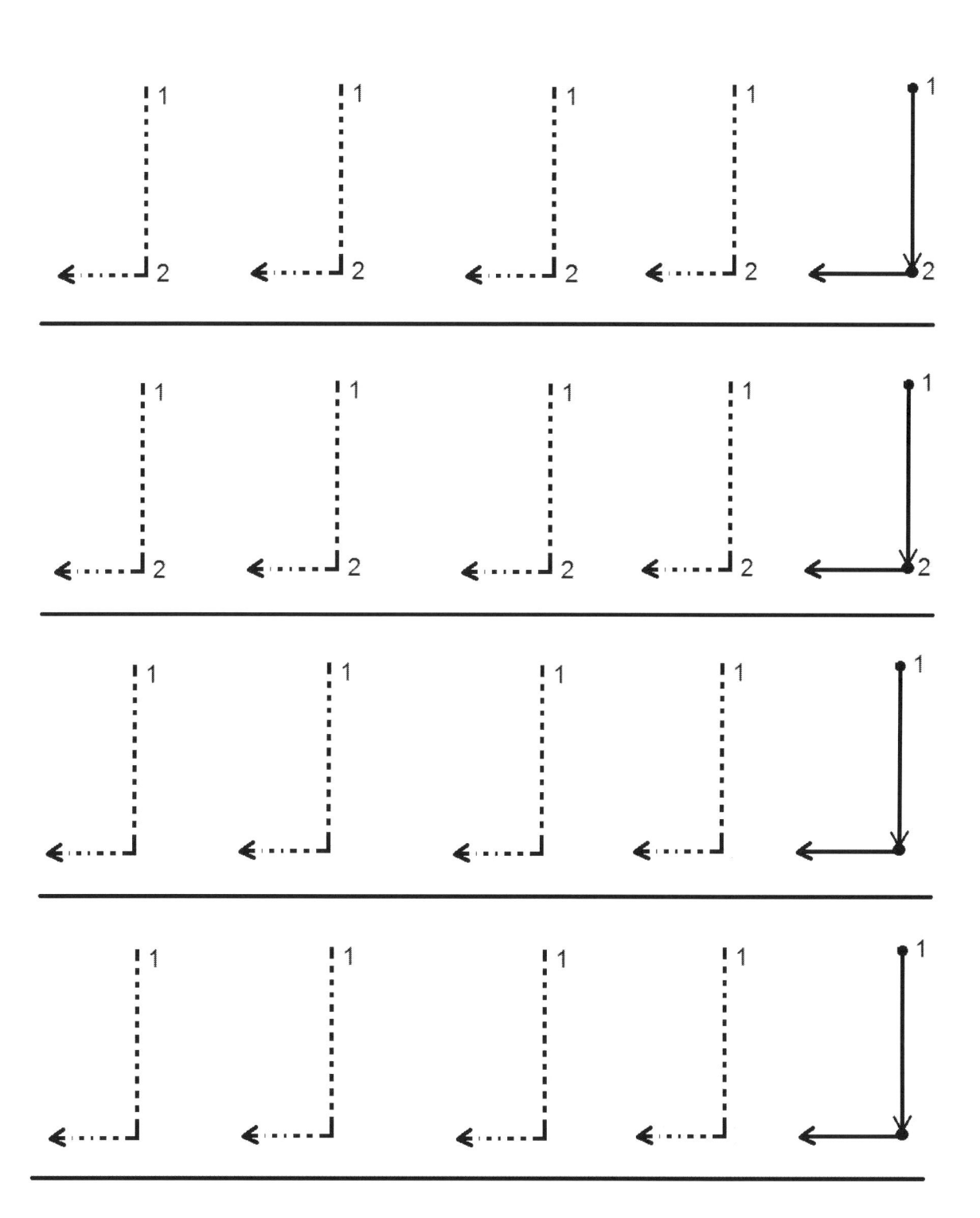

Nun ⟂

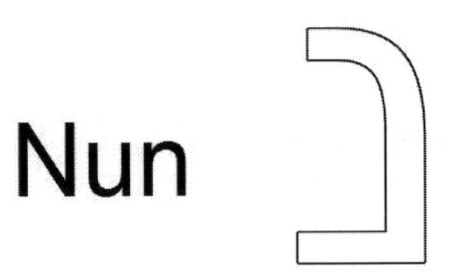

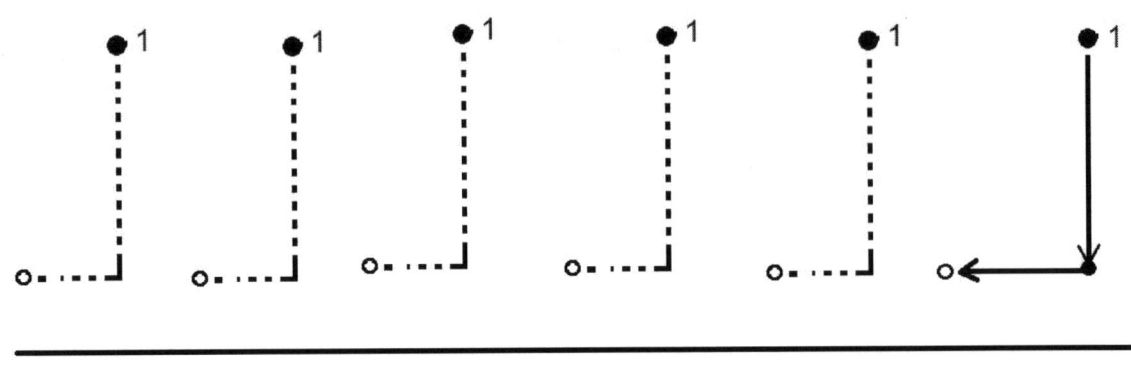

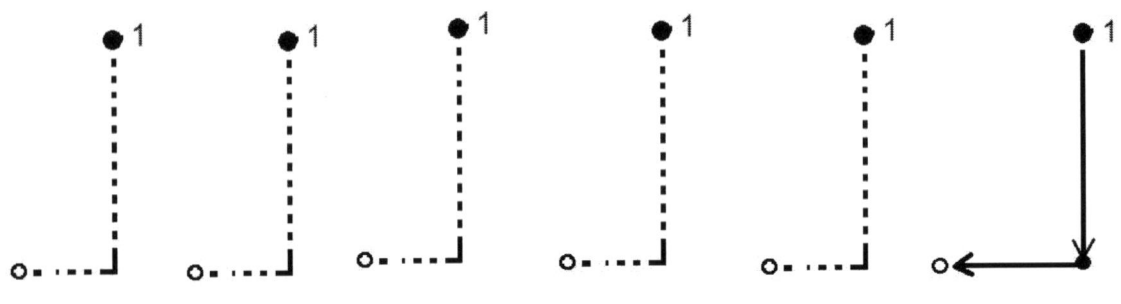

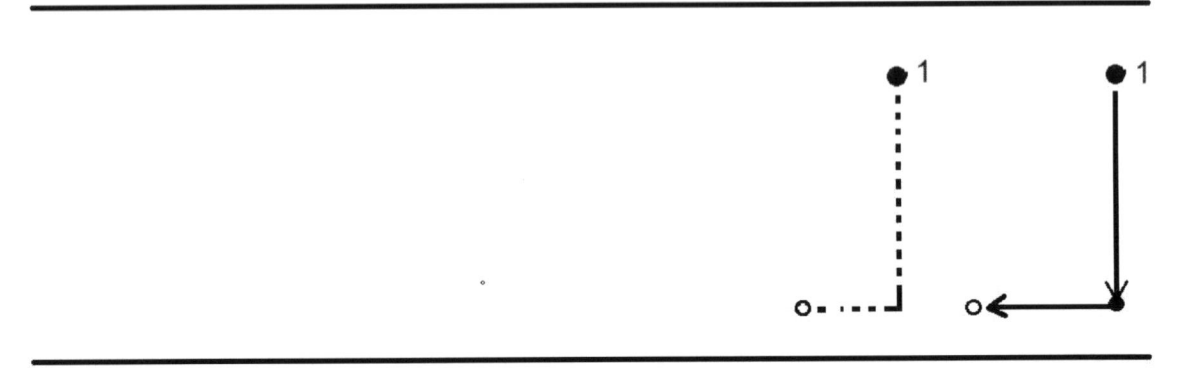

Nun ⌐

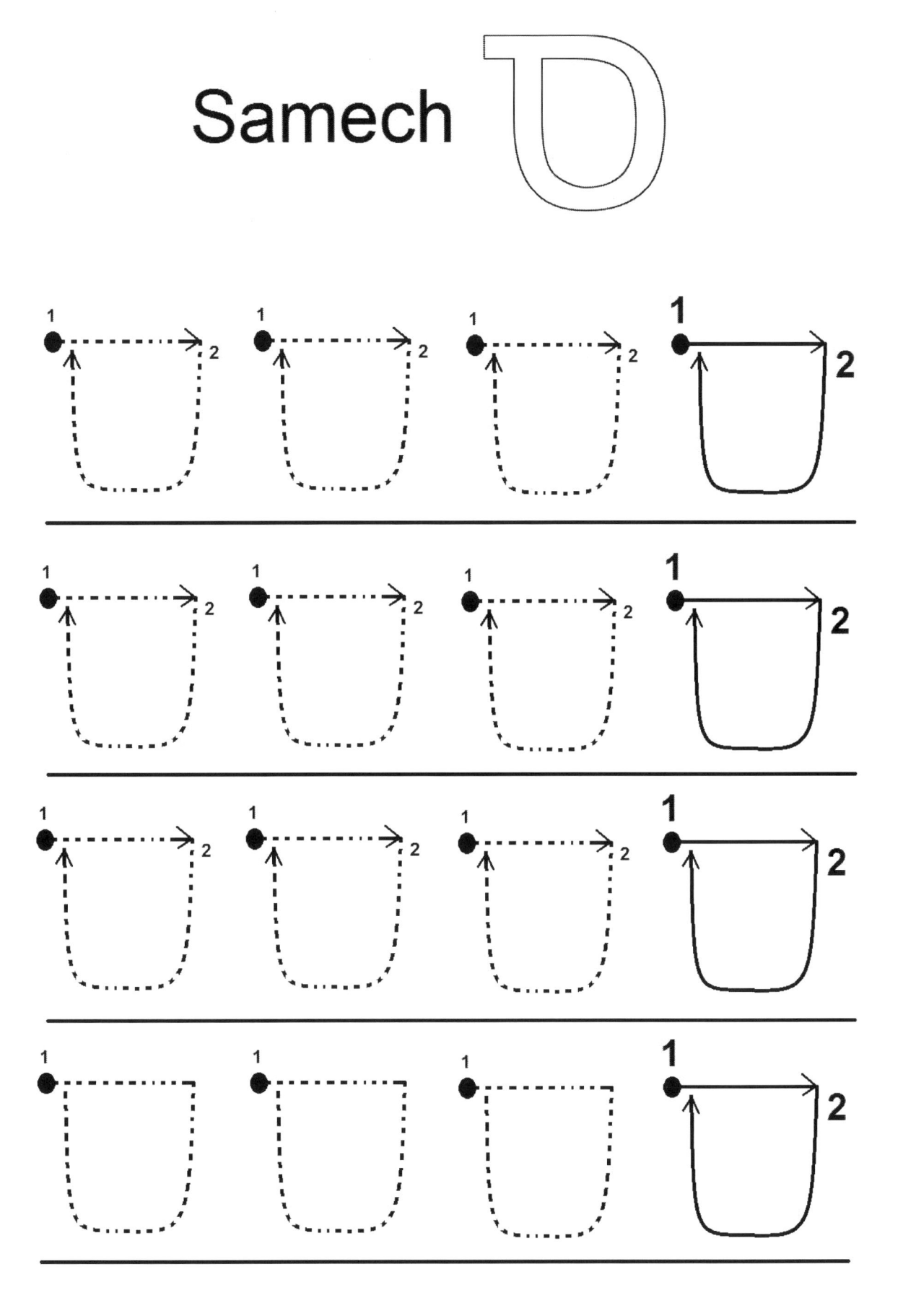

Samech

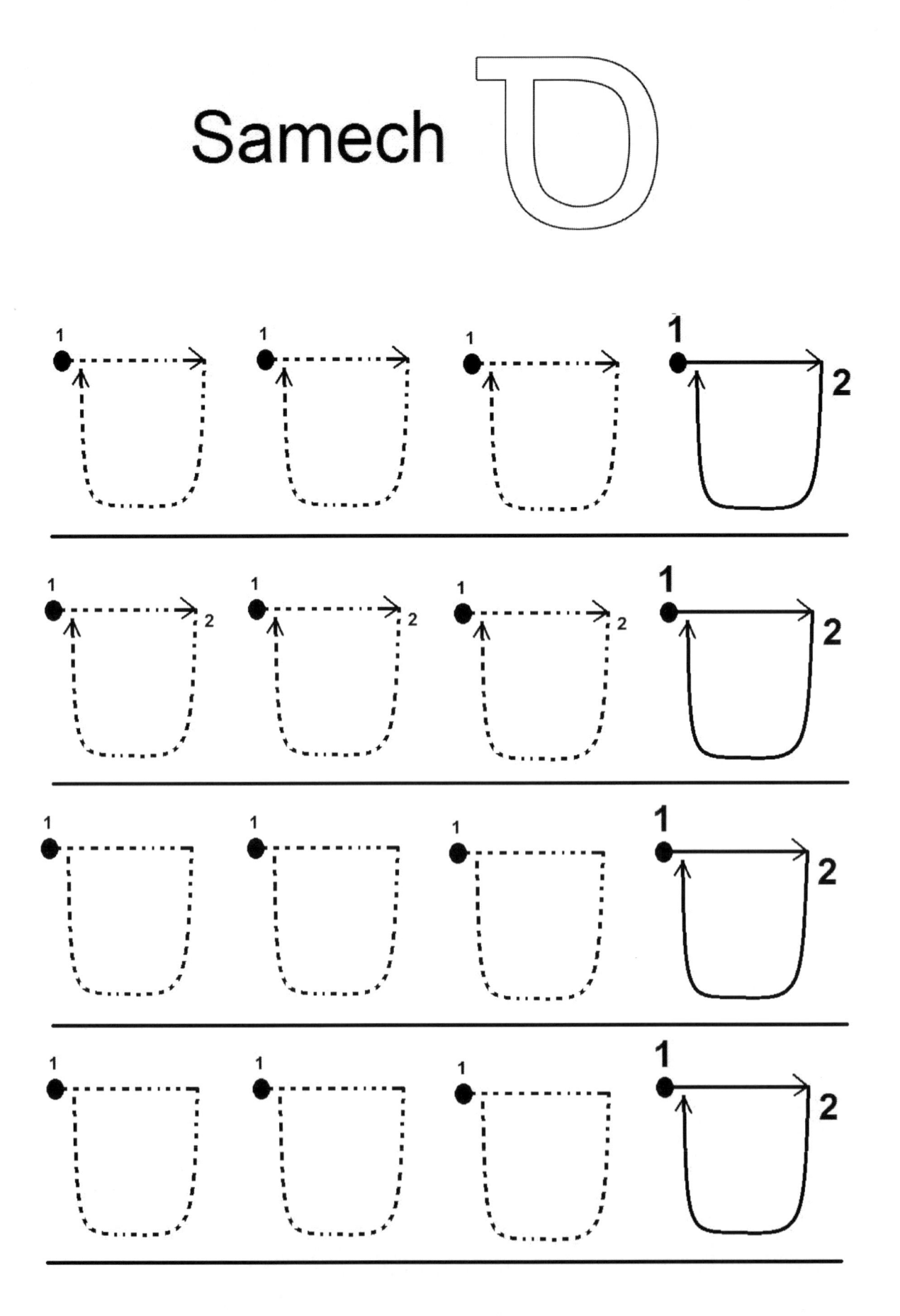

Samech

Samech ס

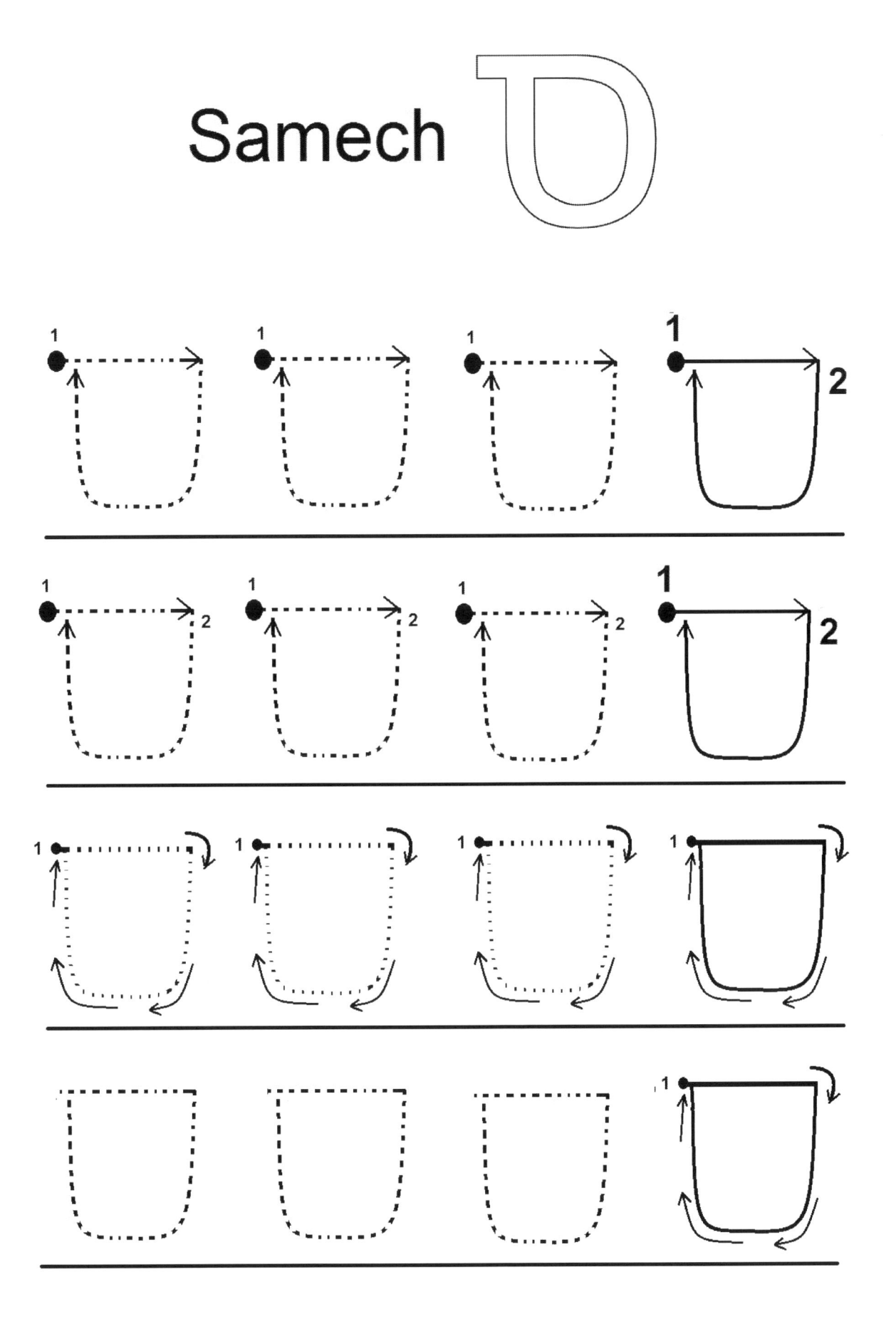

ד	ג	ב	א ←
Dalet	Gimmel	Bet	Aleph

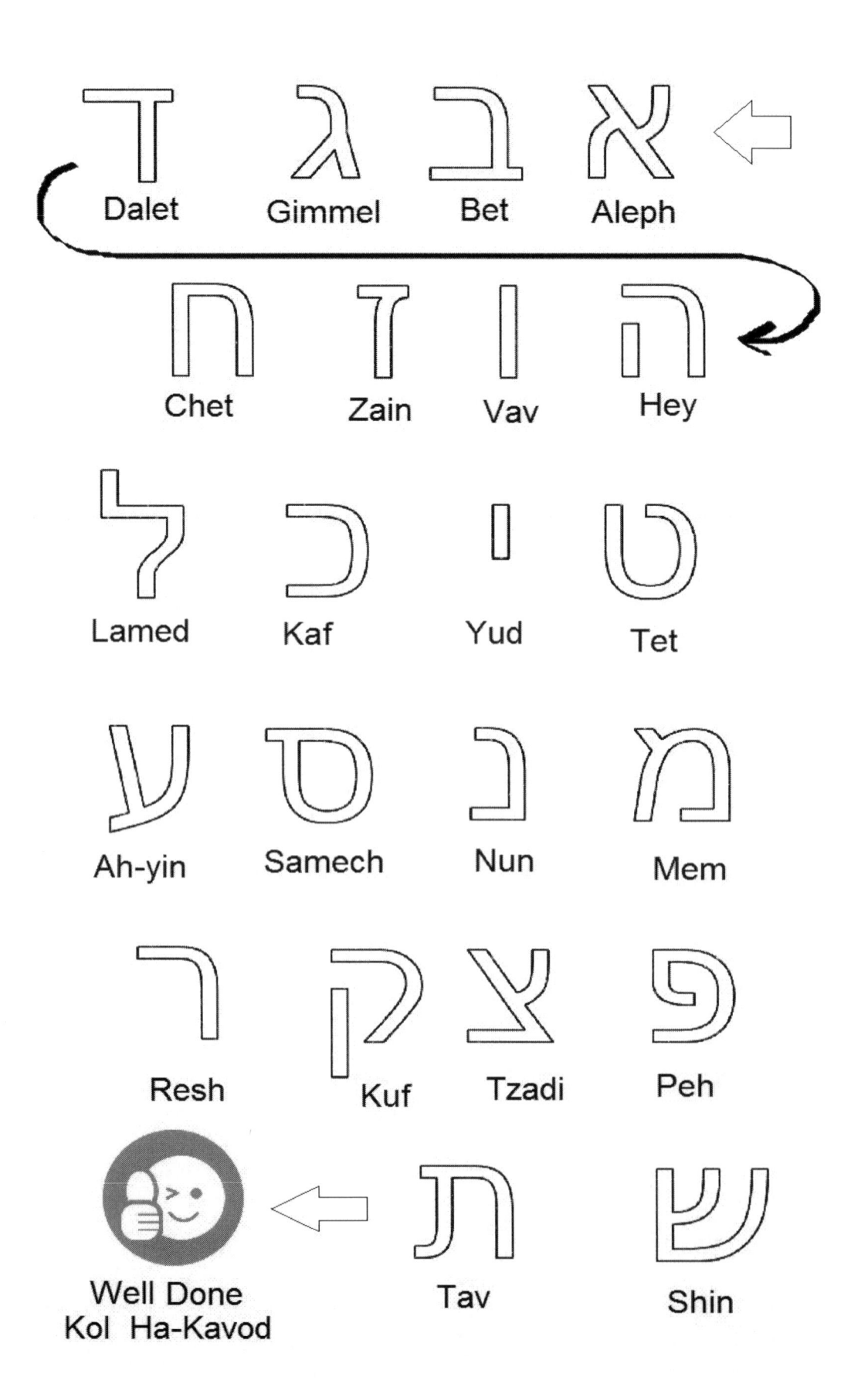

ח	ז	ו	ה
Chet	Zain	Vav	Hey

ל	כ	י	ט
Lamed	Kaf	Yud	Tet

ע	ס	נ	מ
Ah-yin	Samech	Nun	Mem

ר	ק	צ	פ
Resh	Kuf	Tzadi	Peh

		ת	ש
Well Done Kol Ha-Kavod		Tav	Shin

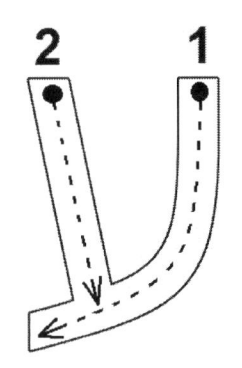

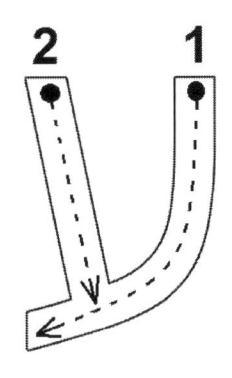

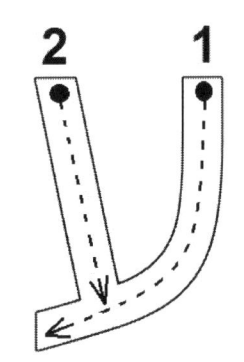

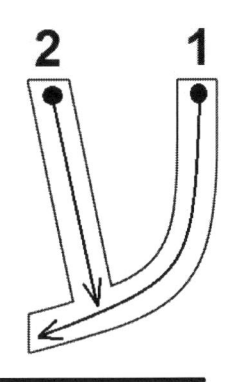

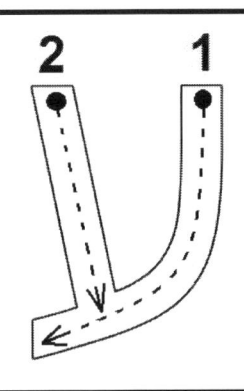

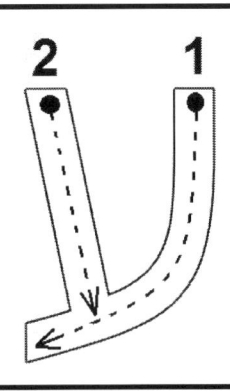

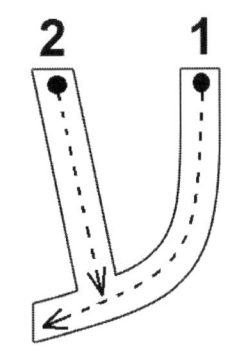

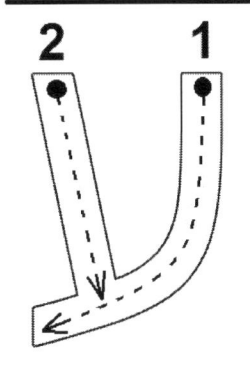

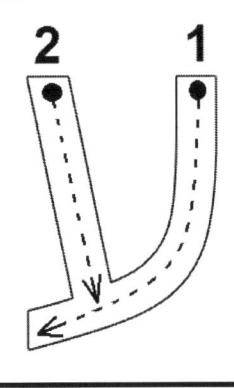

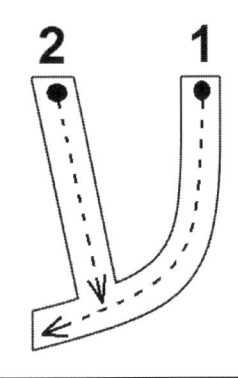

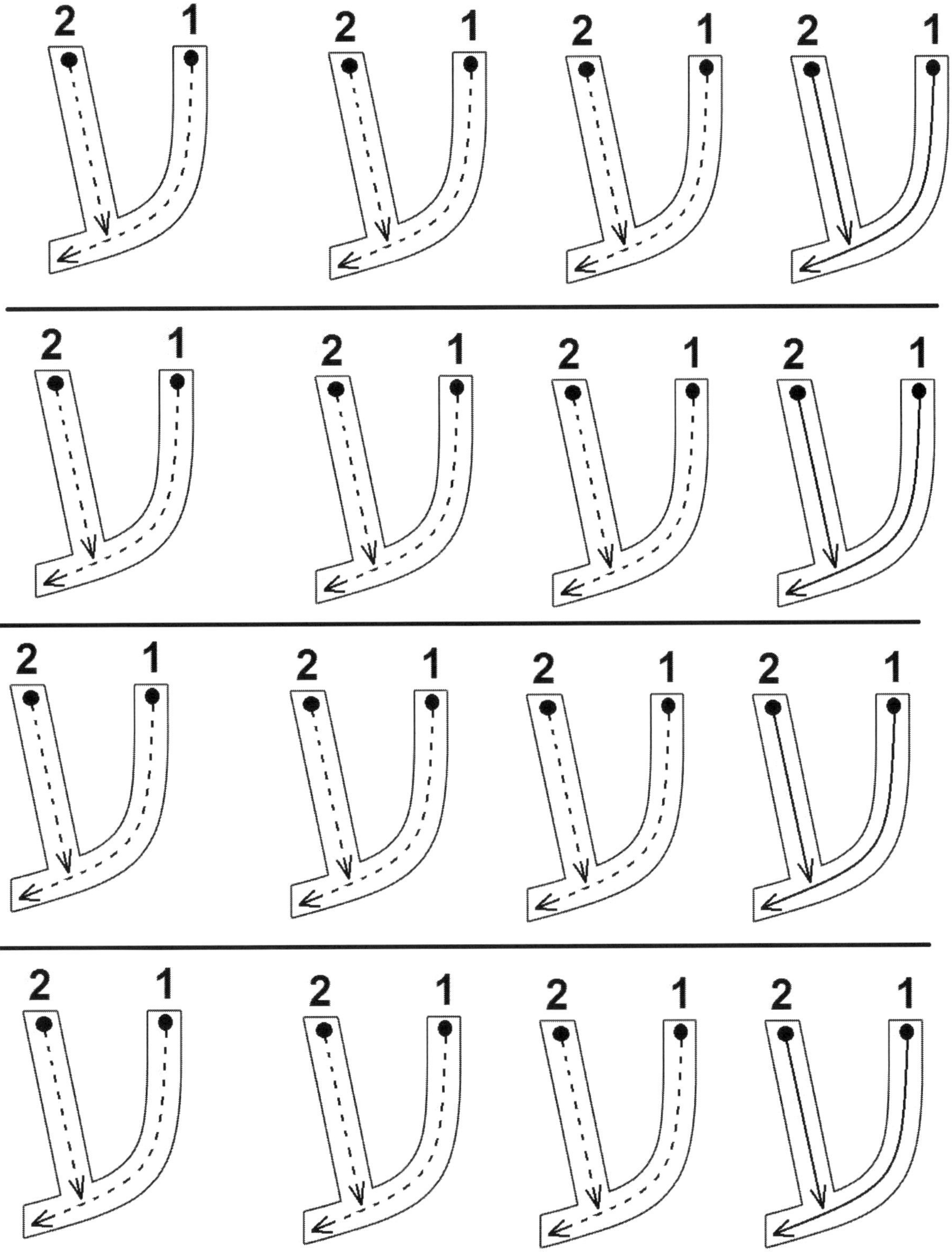

A-yeen

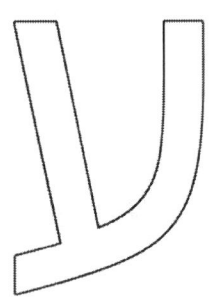

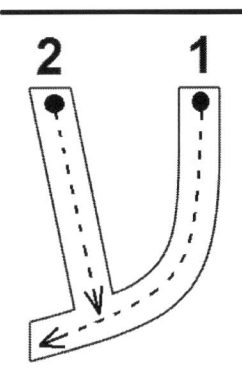

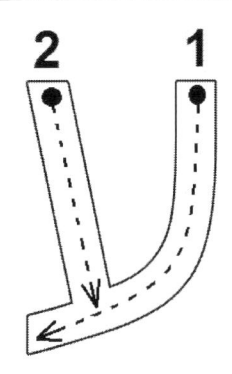

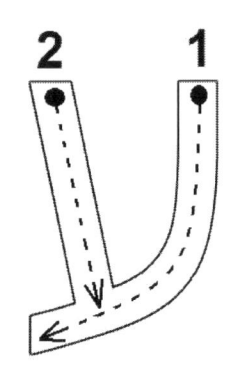

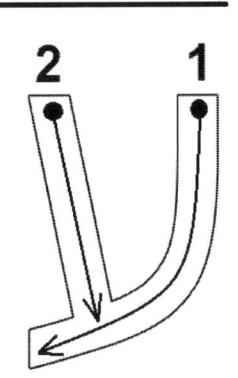

A-yeen

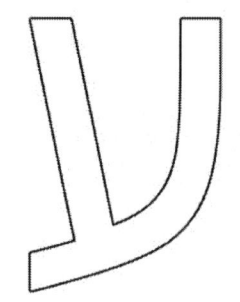

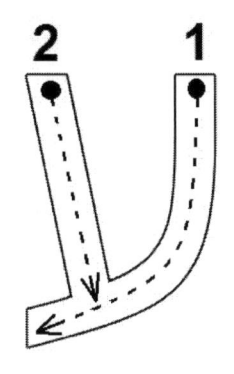

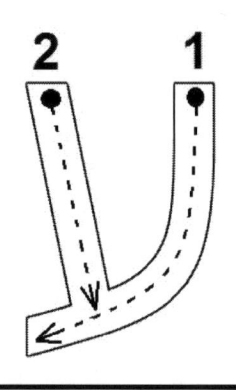

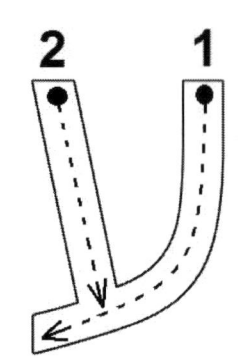

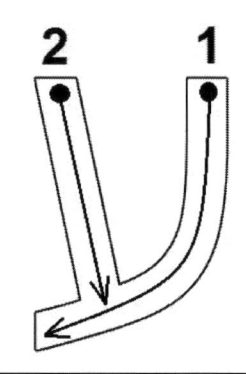

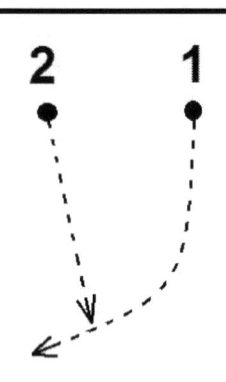

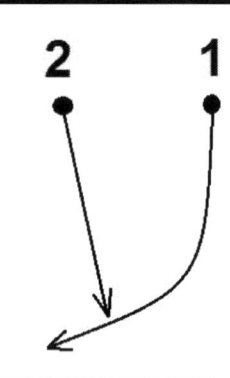

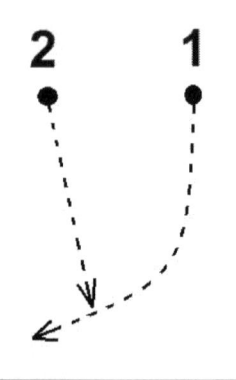

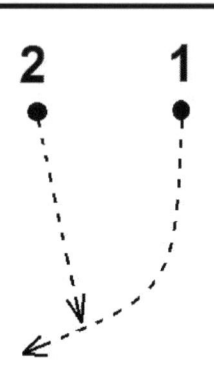

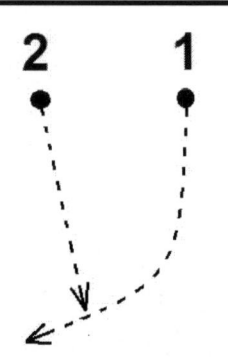

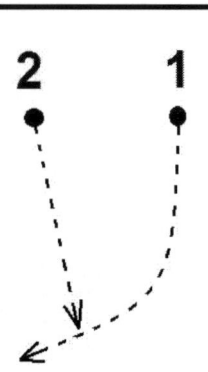

A-yeen

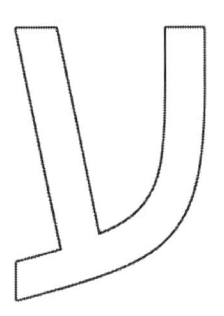

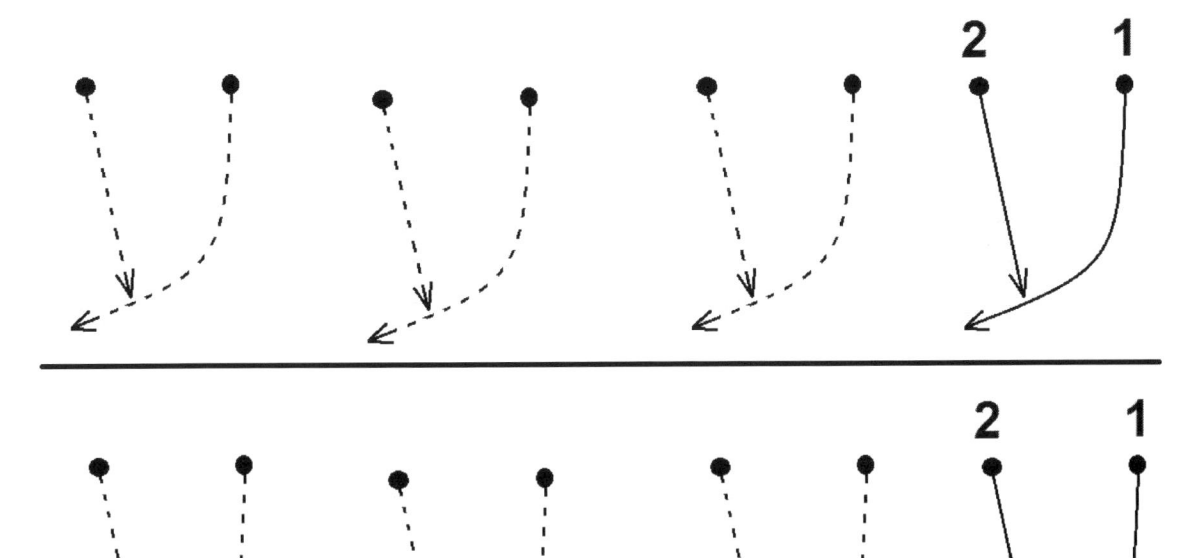

Peh

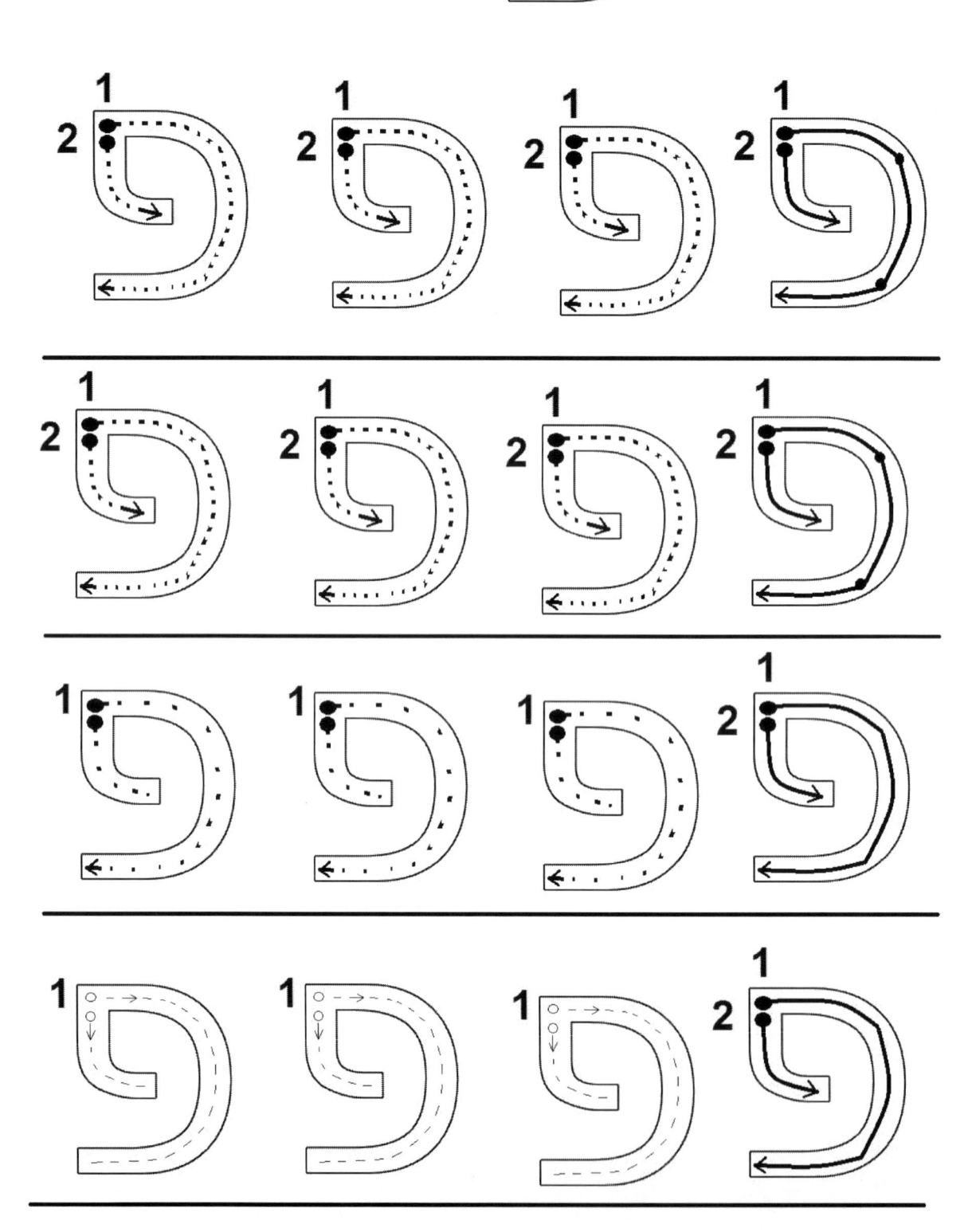

Peh

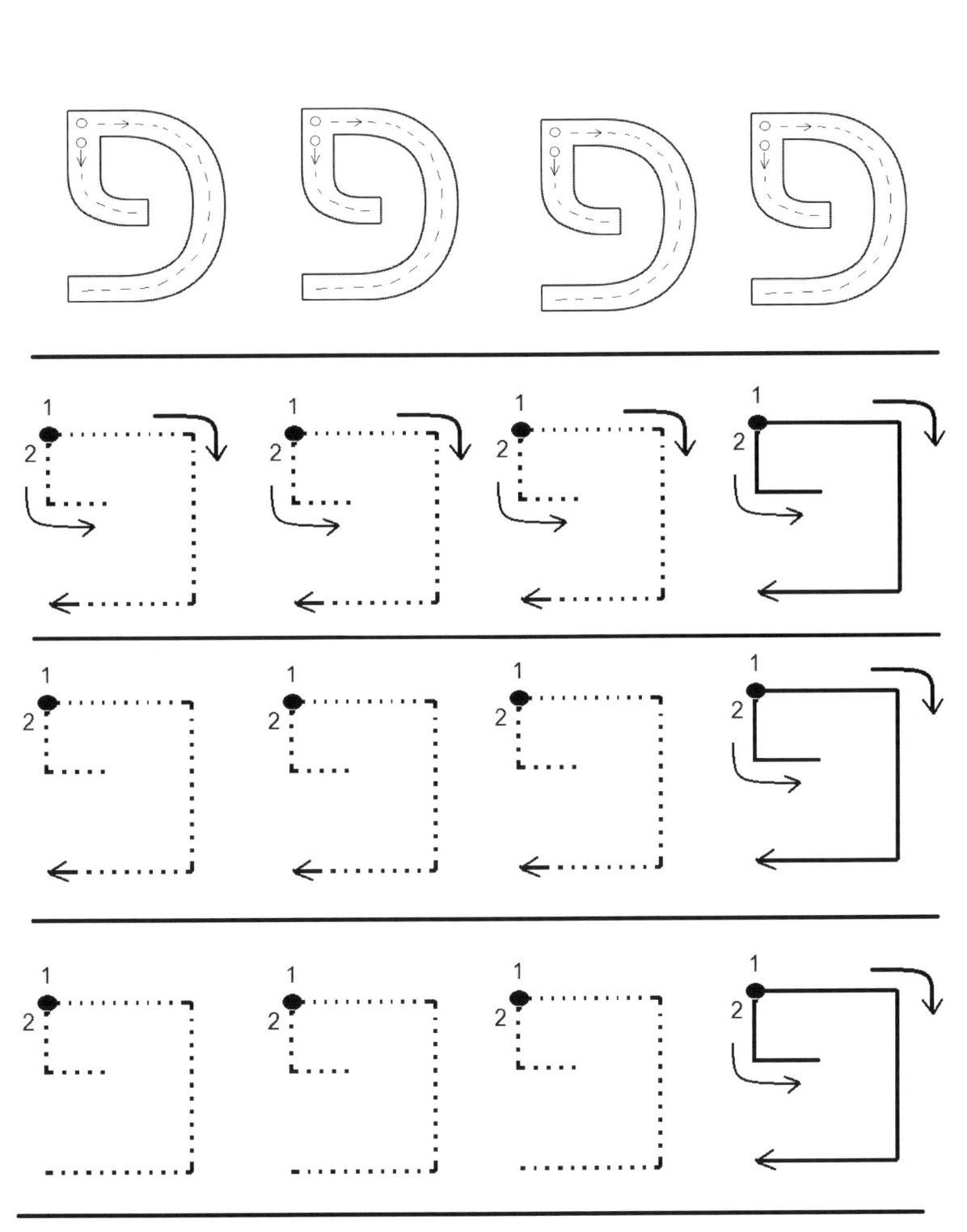

Peh

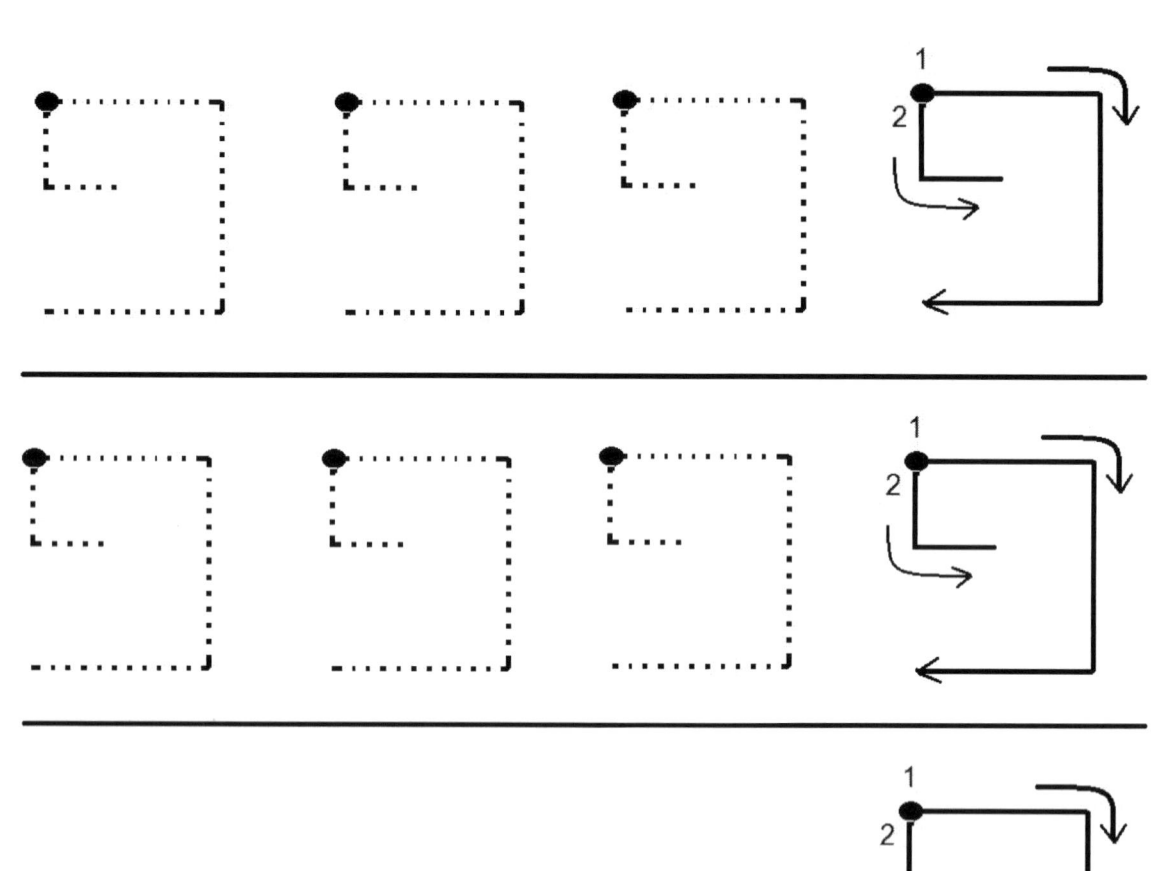

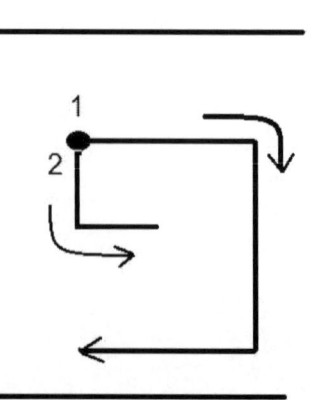

Peh

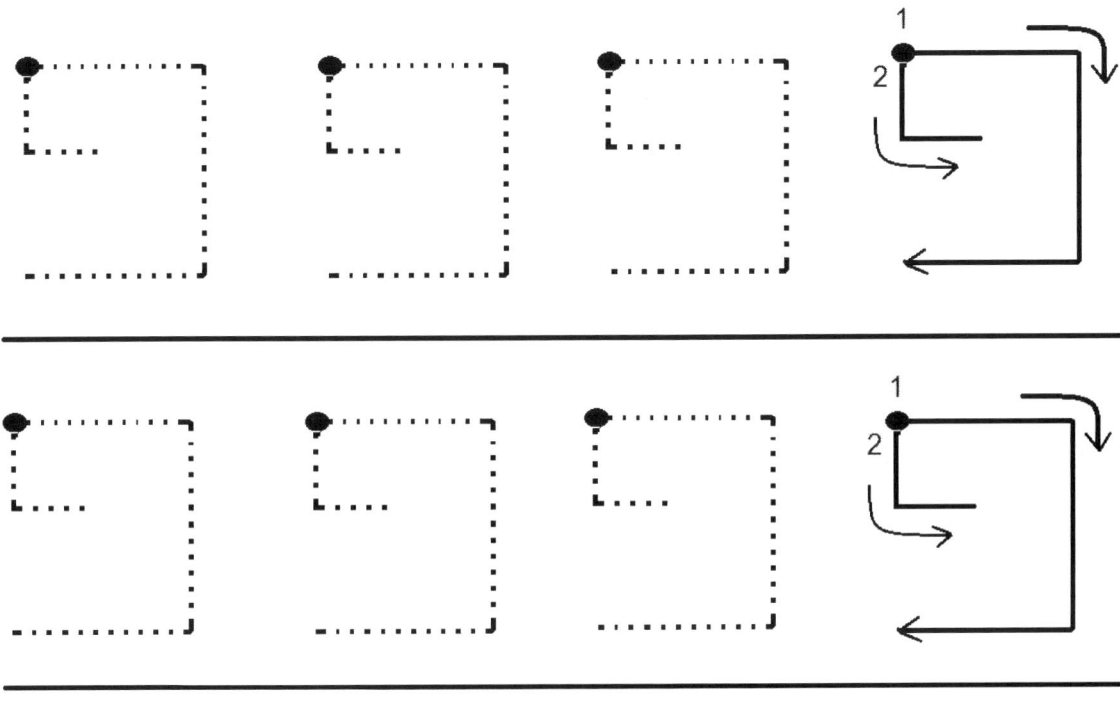

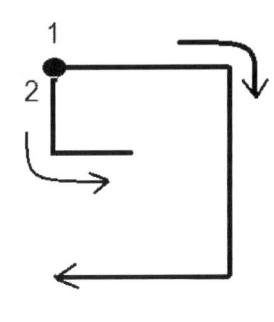

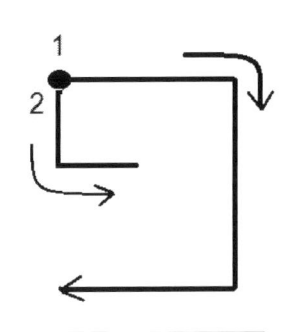

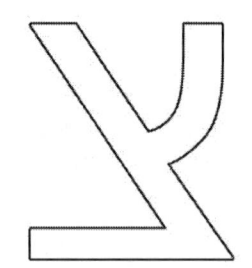

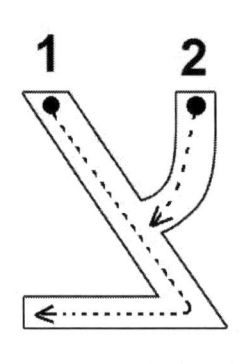

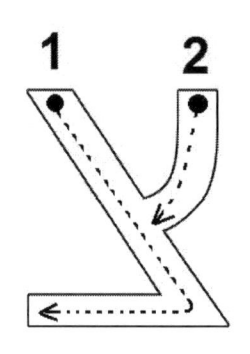

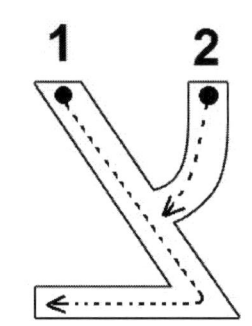

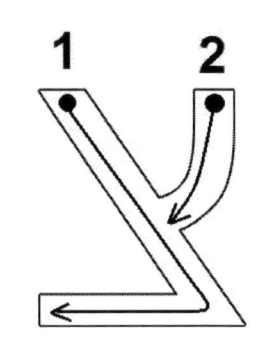

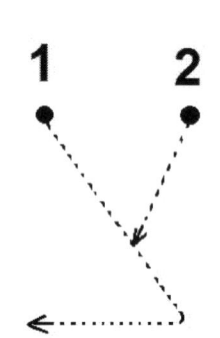

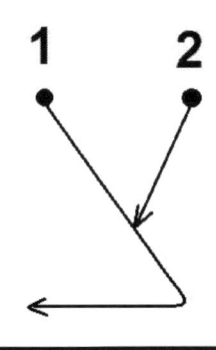

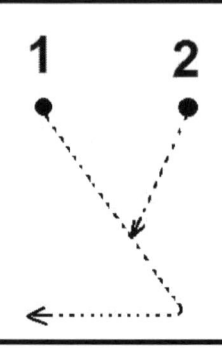

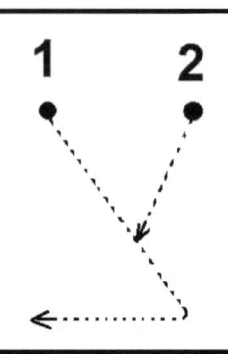

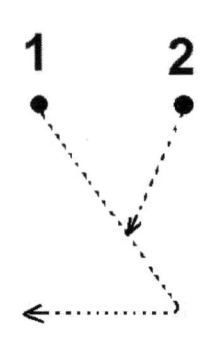

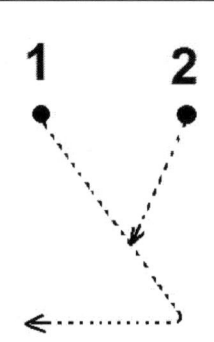

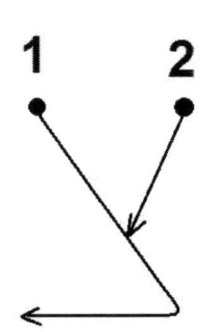

Tza-di

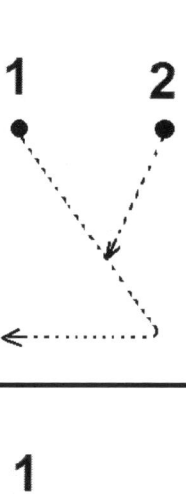

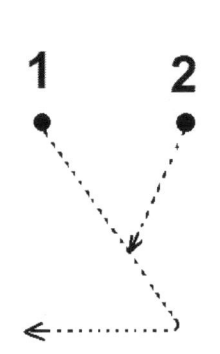

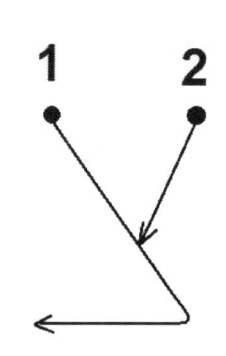

Tza-di

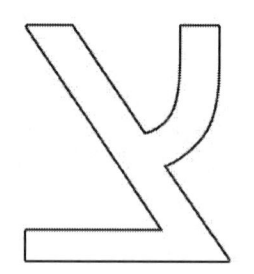

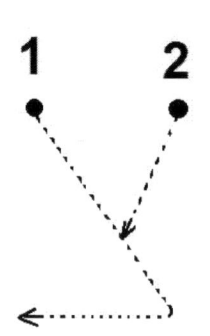

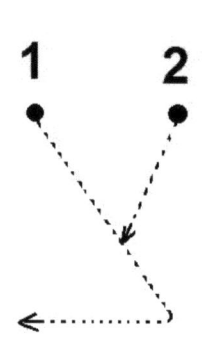

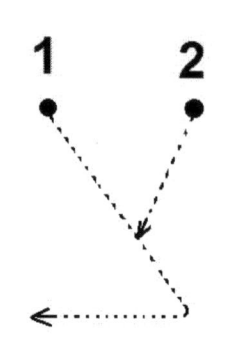

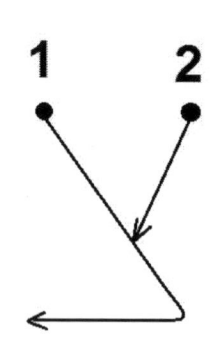

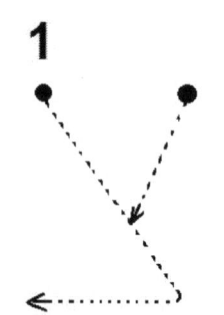

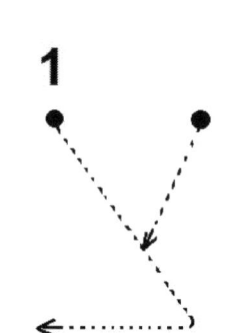

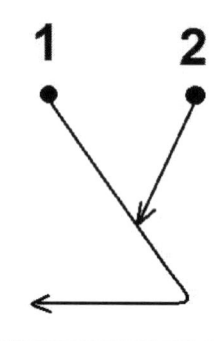

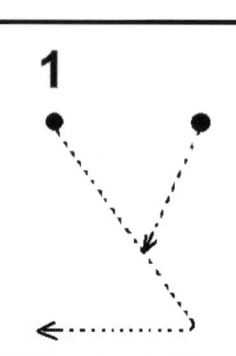

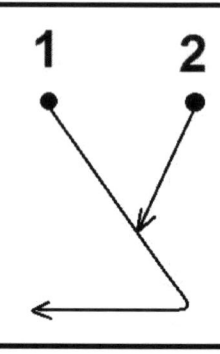

Tza-di

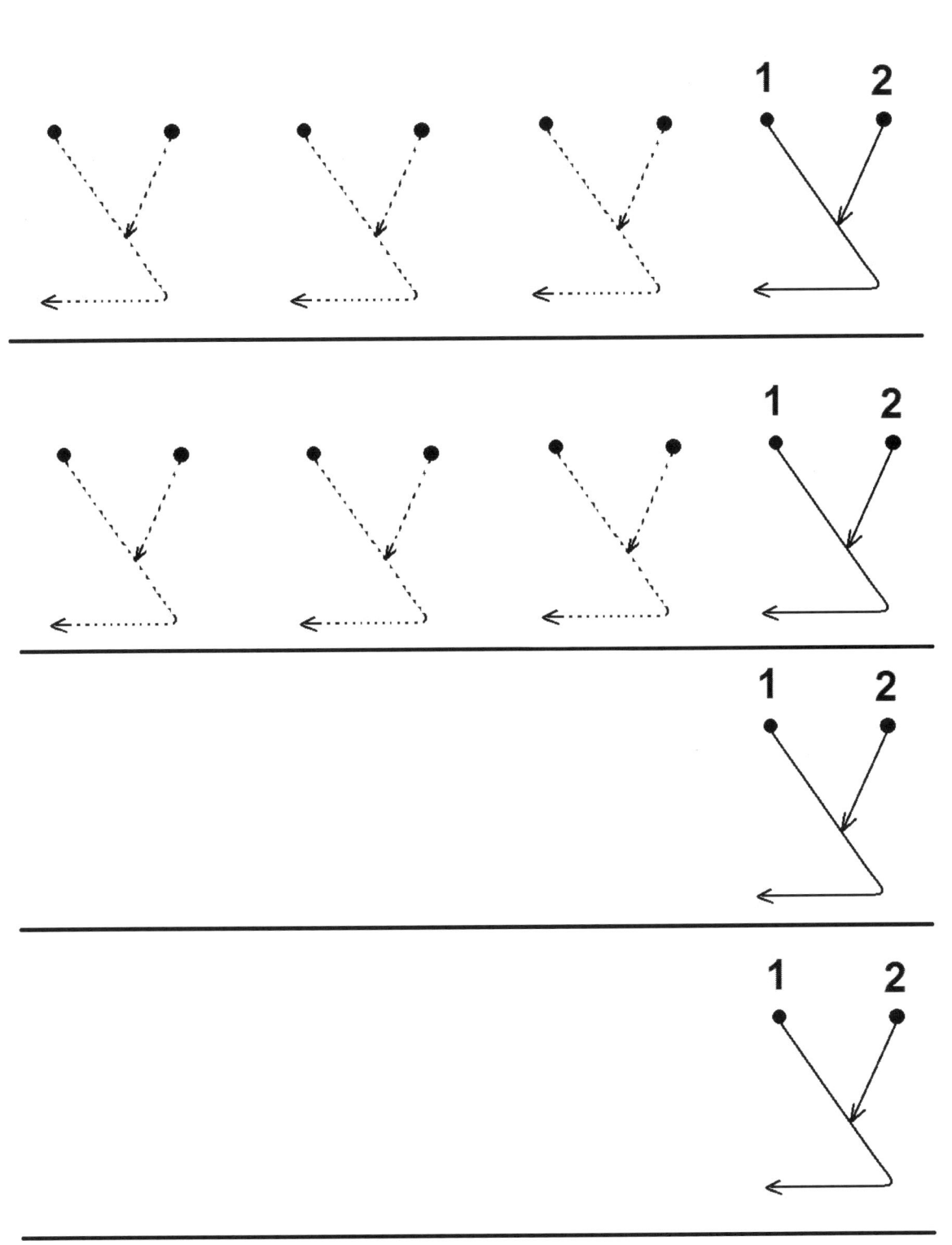

Tza-di

ד	ג	ב	א
Dalet	Gimmel	Bet	Aleph

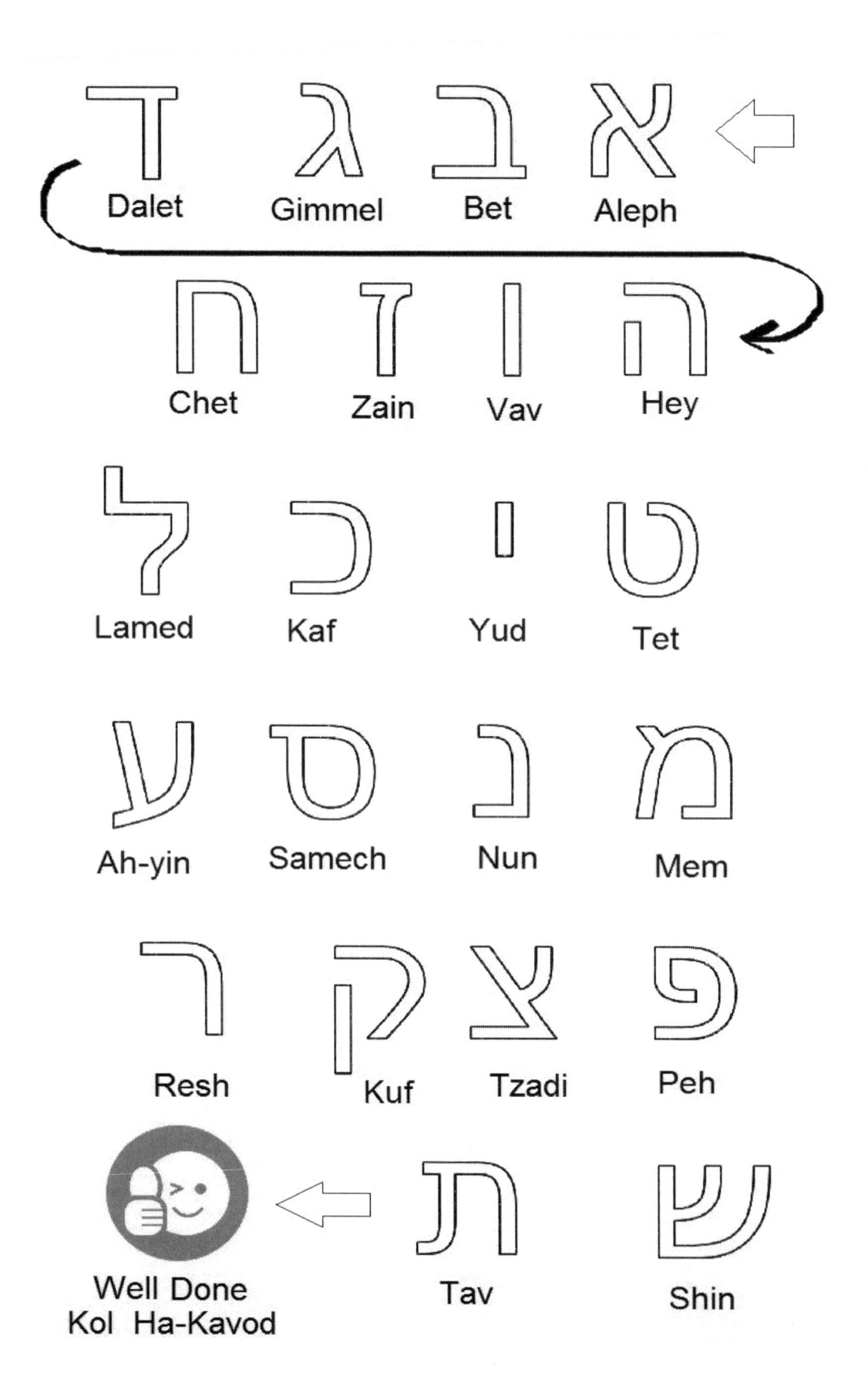

ח	ז	ו	ה
Chet	Zain	Vav	Hey

ל	כ	י	ט
Lamed	Kaf	Yud	Tet

ע	ס	נ	מ
Ah-yin	Samech	Nun	Mem

ר	ק	צ	פ
Resh	Kuf	Tzadi	Peh

ת	ש
Tav	Shin

Well Done
Kol Ha-Kavod

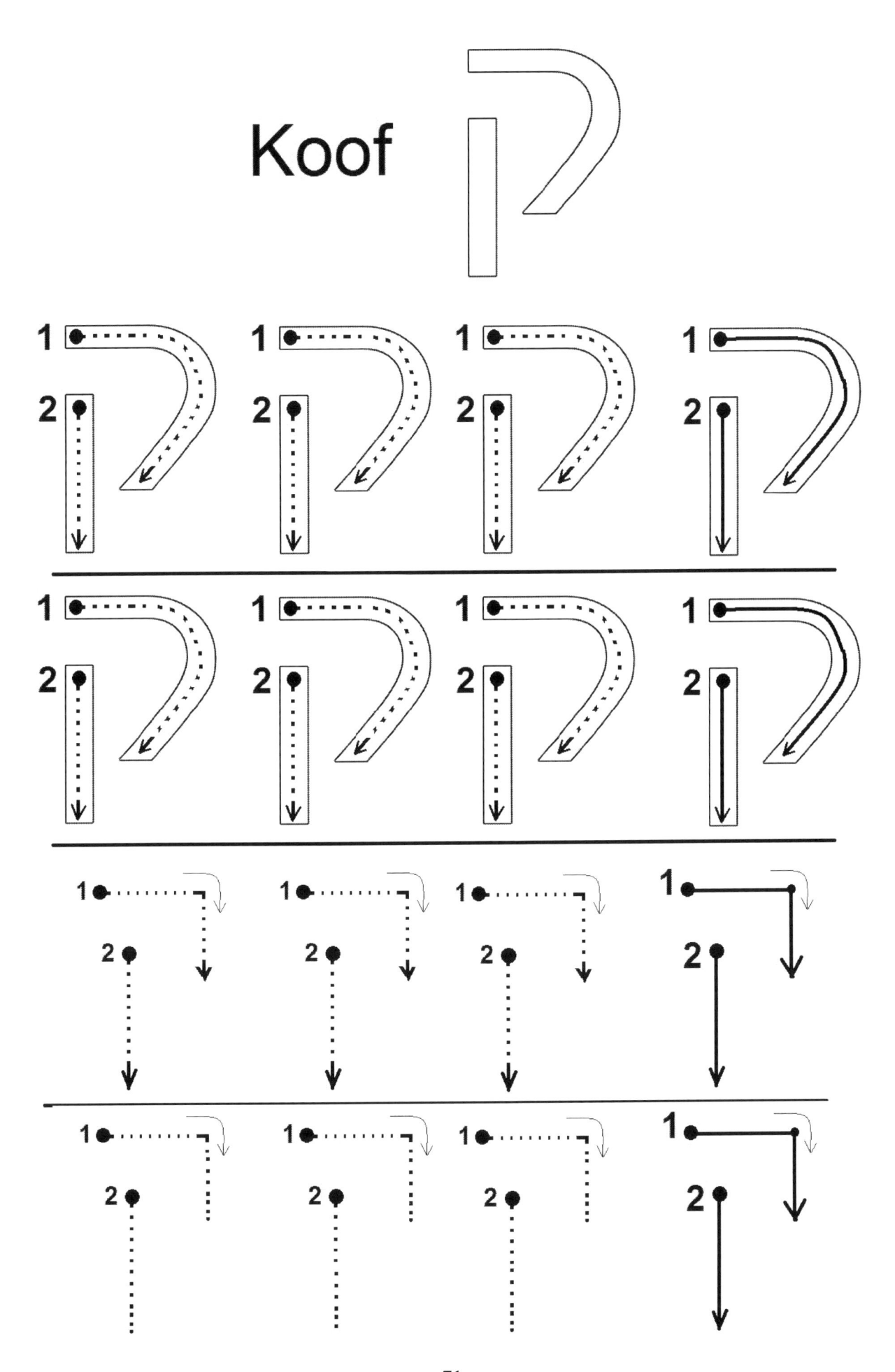

Koof

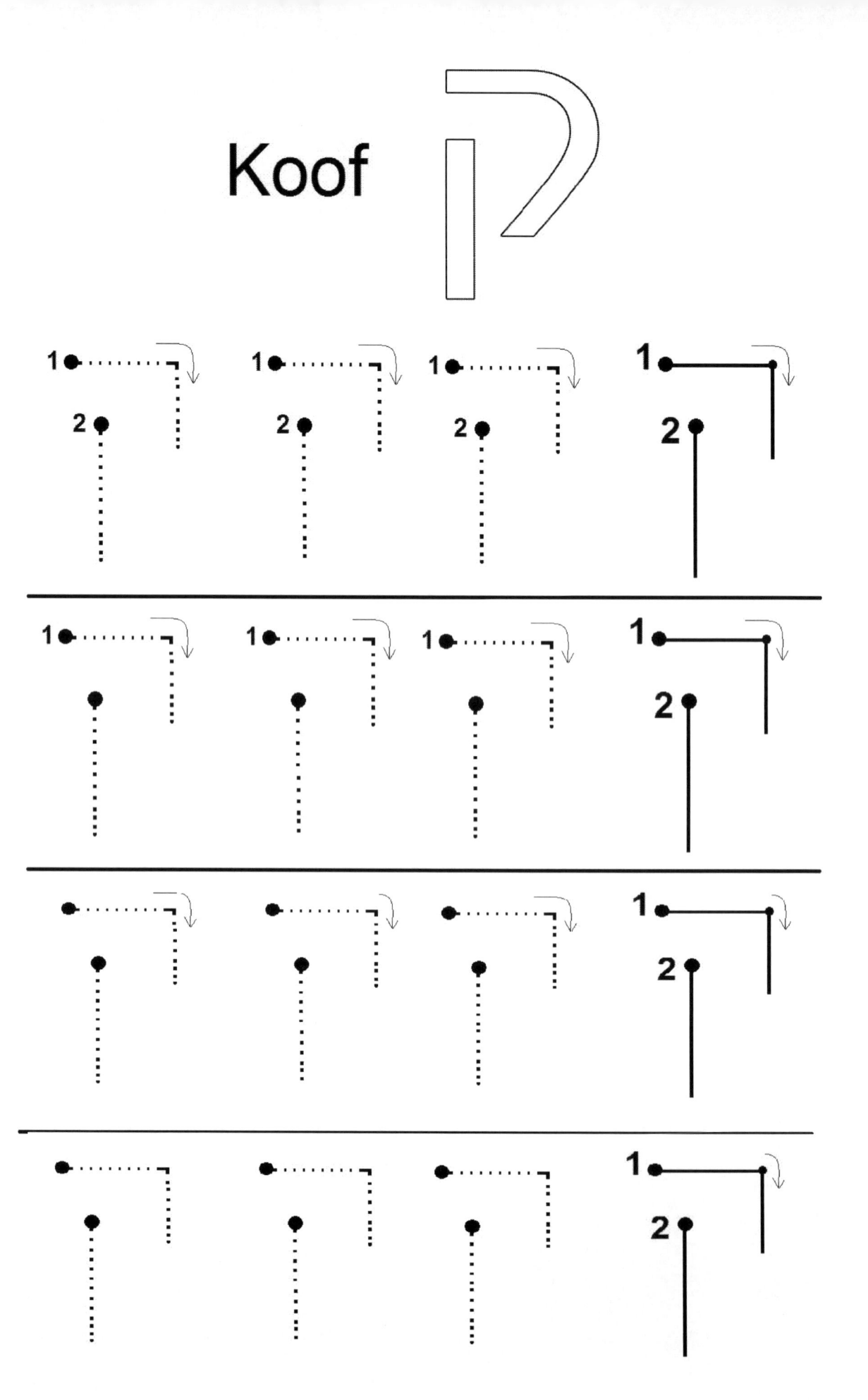

Koof

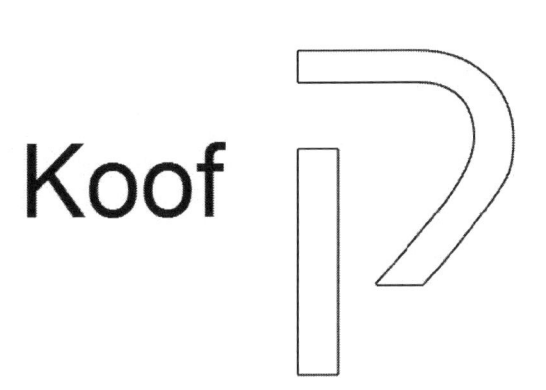

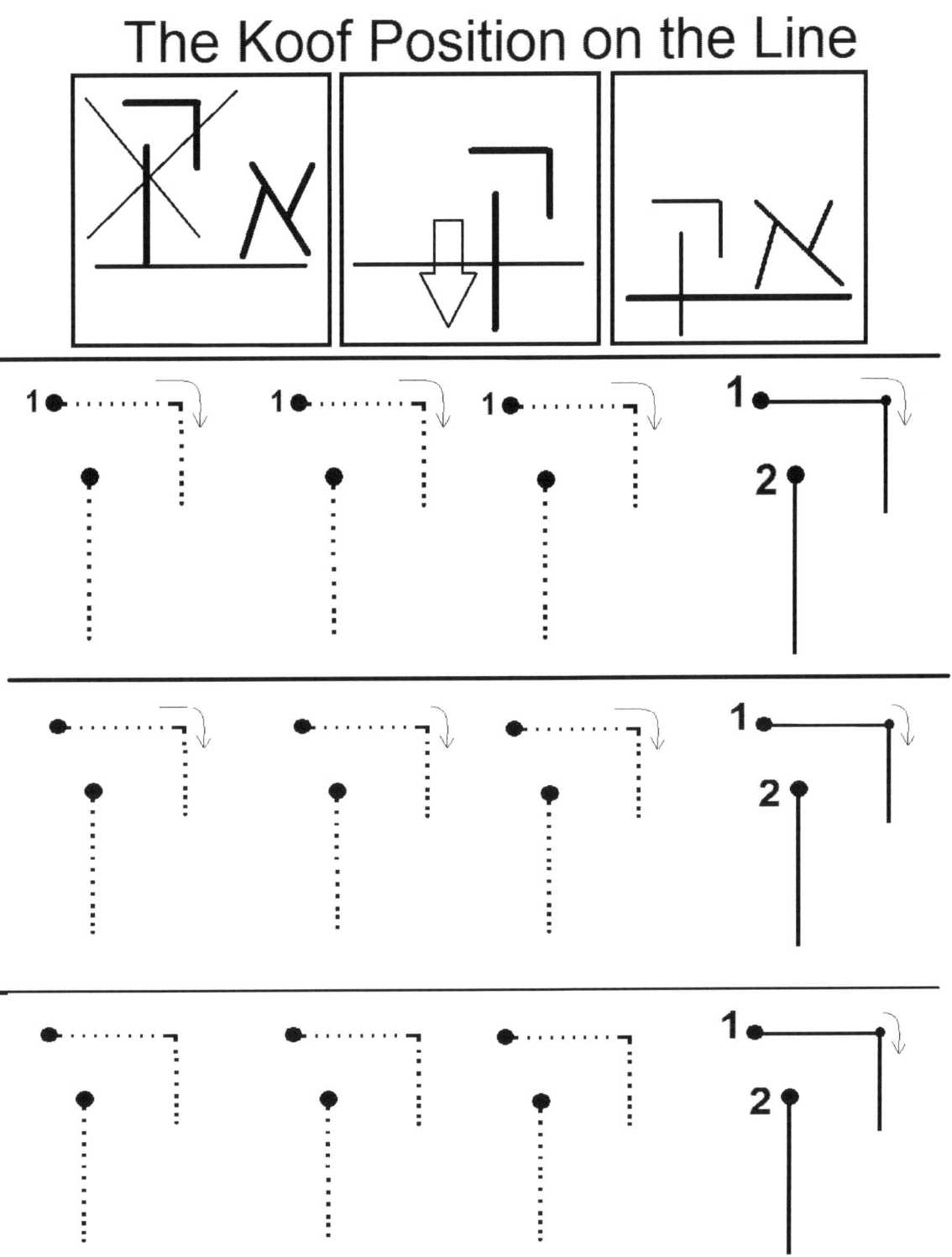

Koof

The Koof Position on the Line

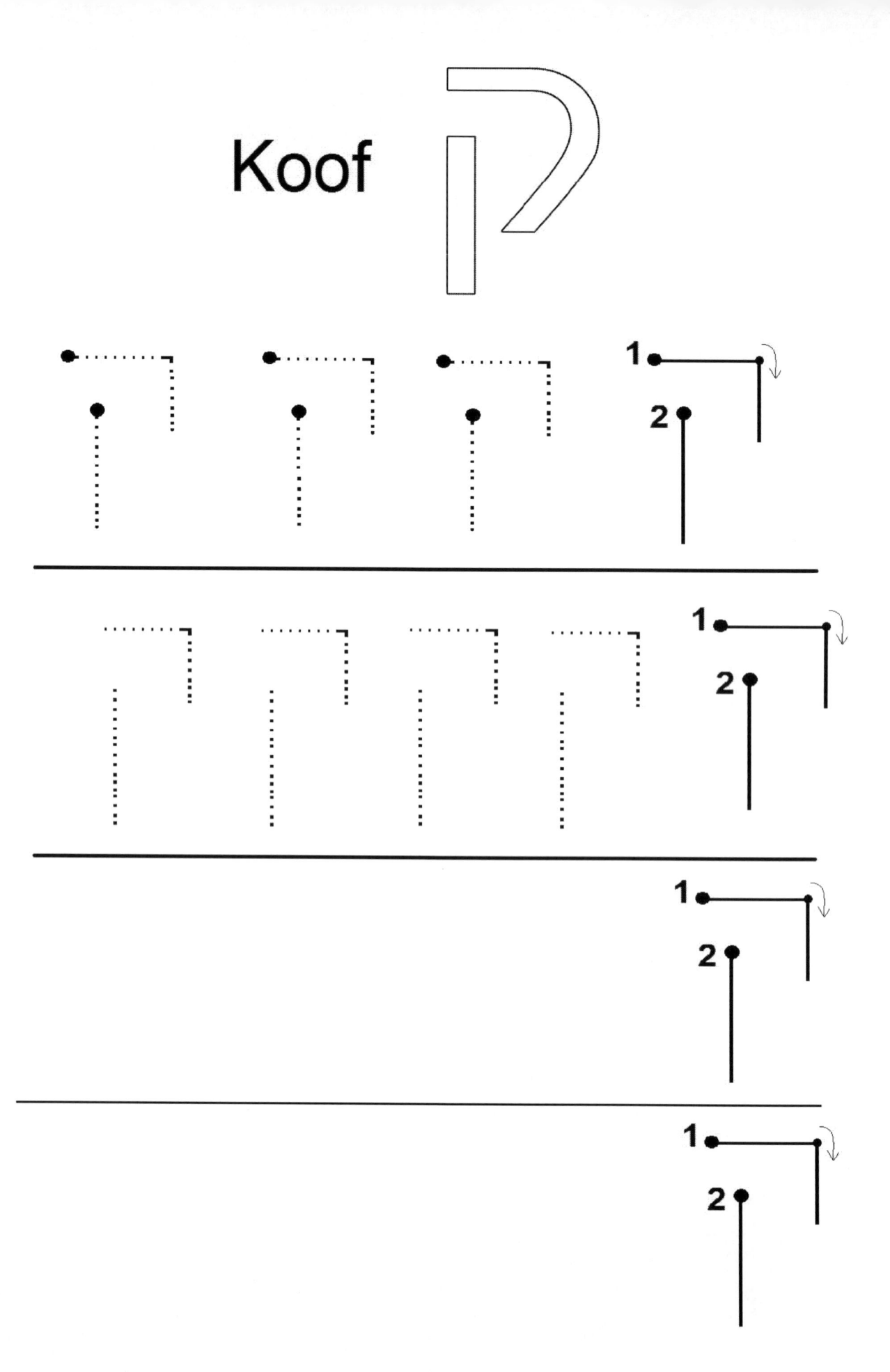

Koof

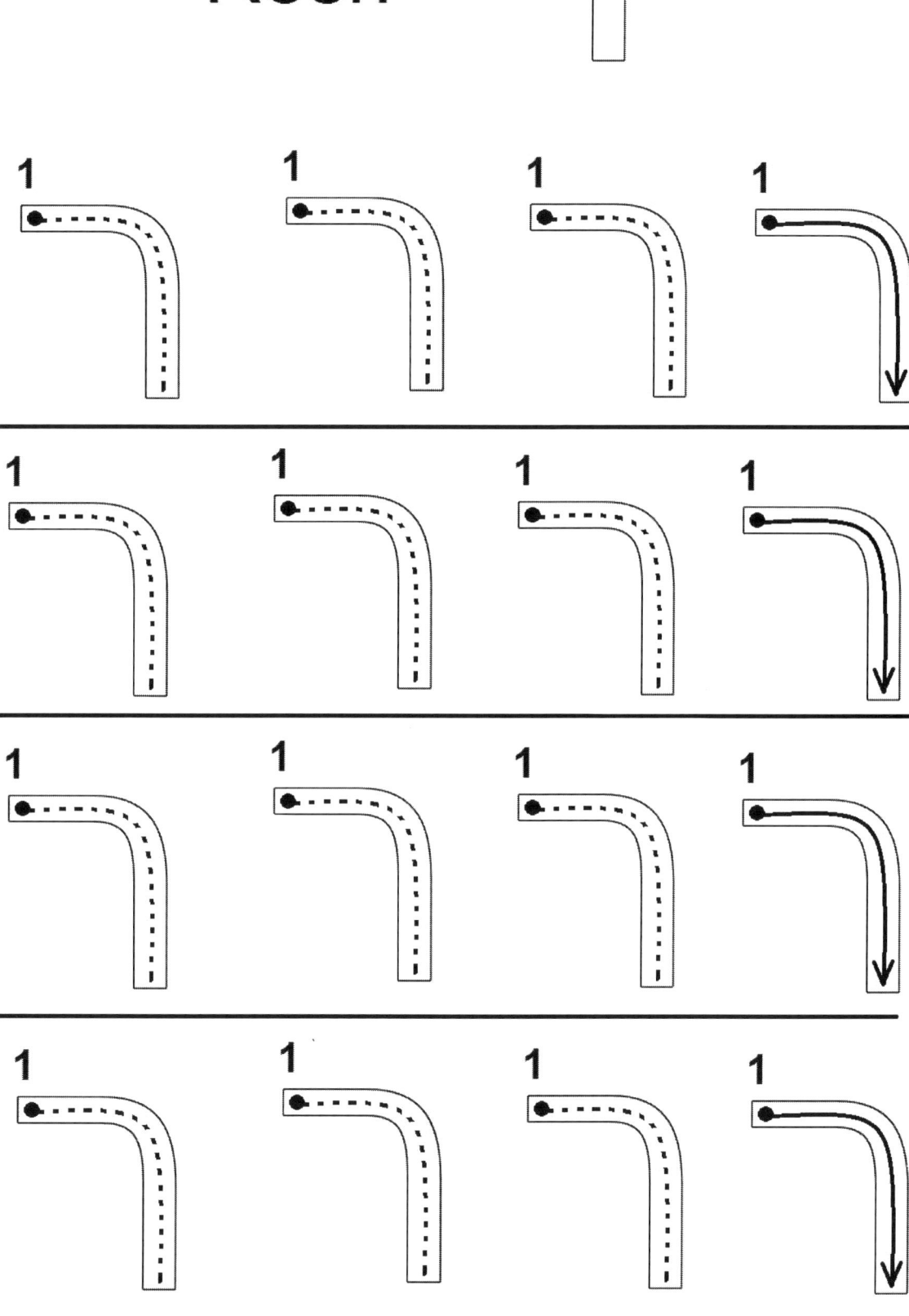

Resh

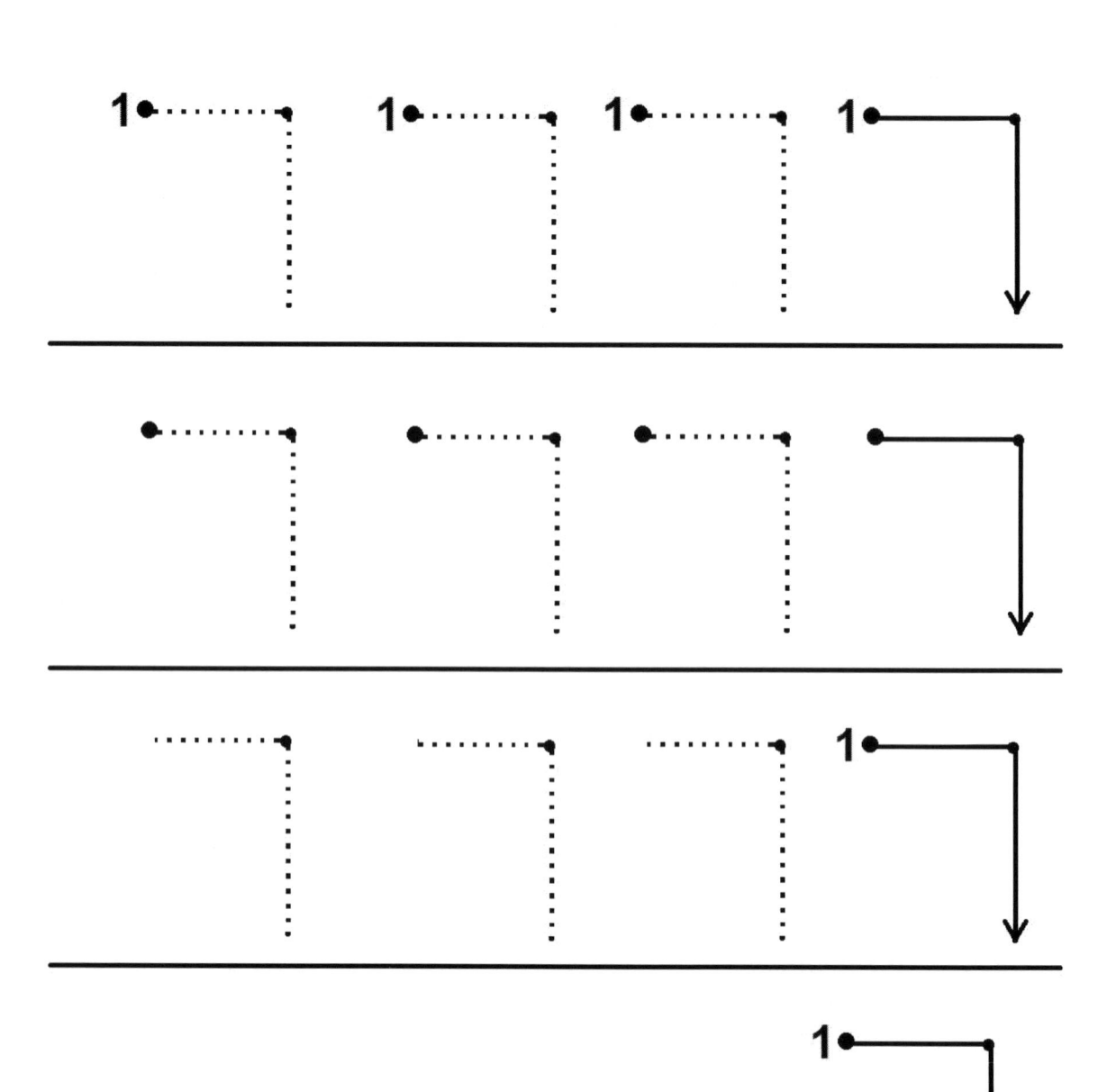

Resh

Shin ש

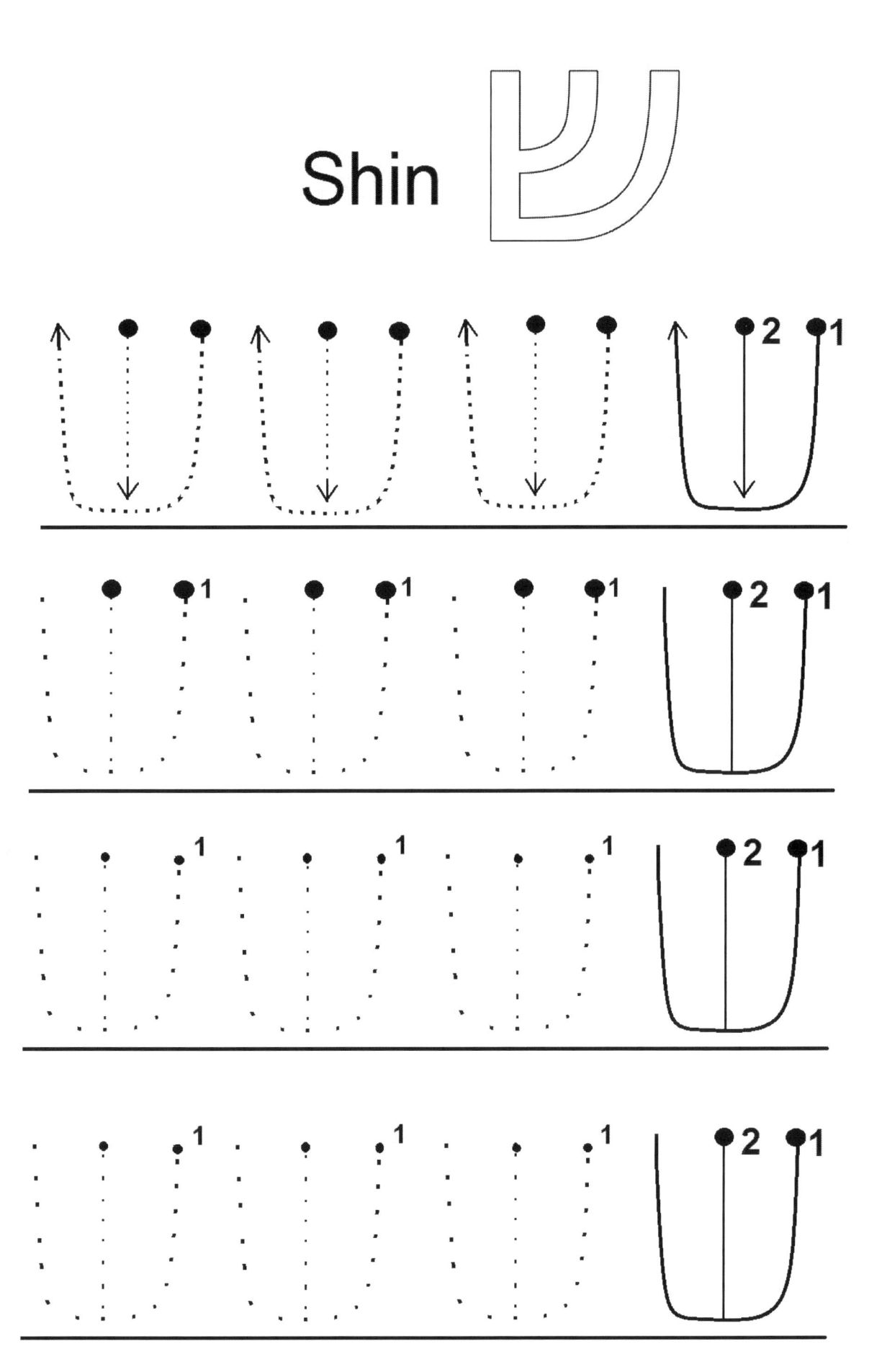

Shin ש

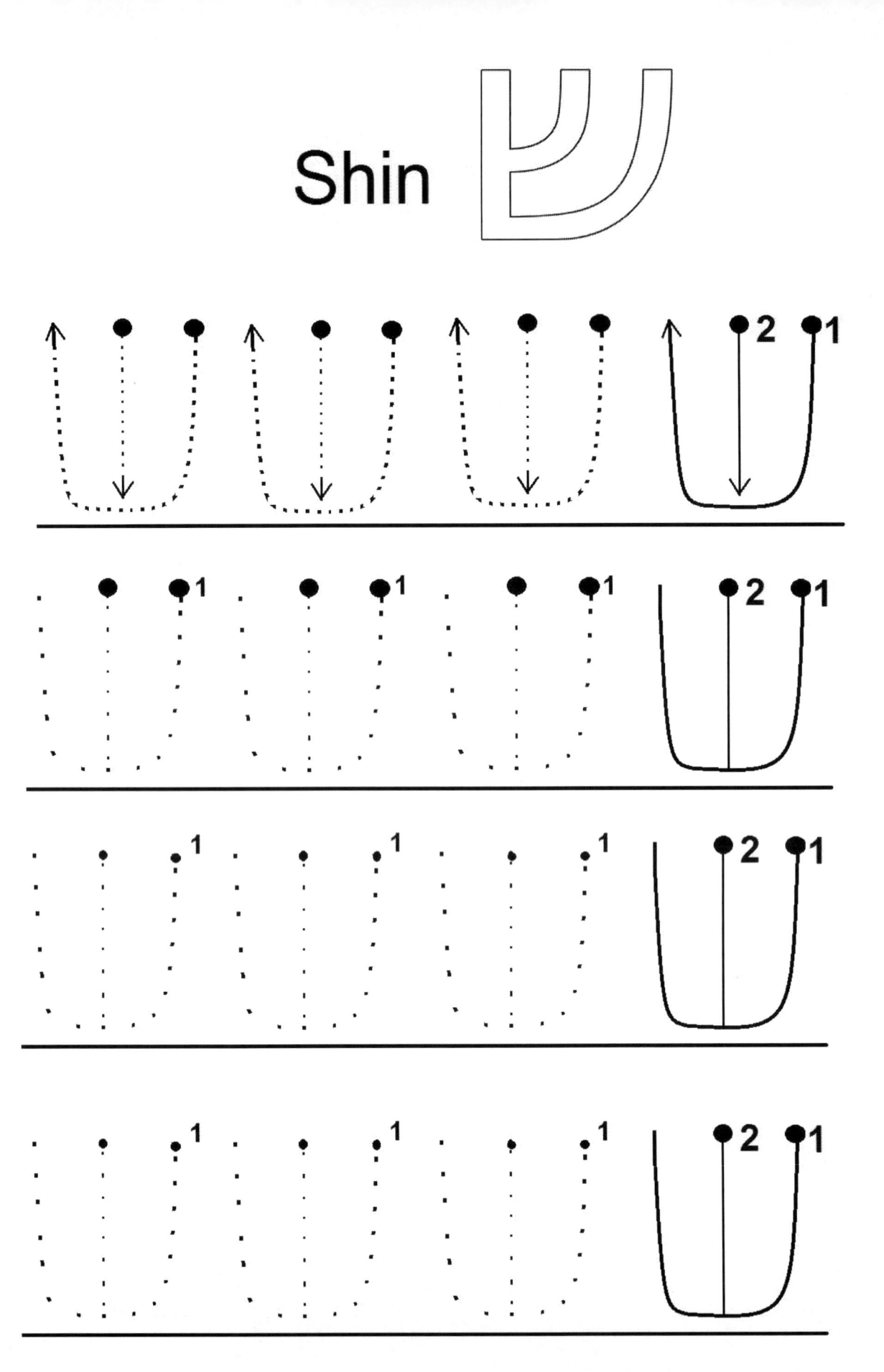

Shin ש

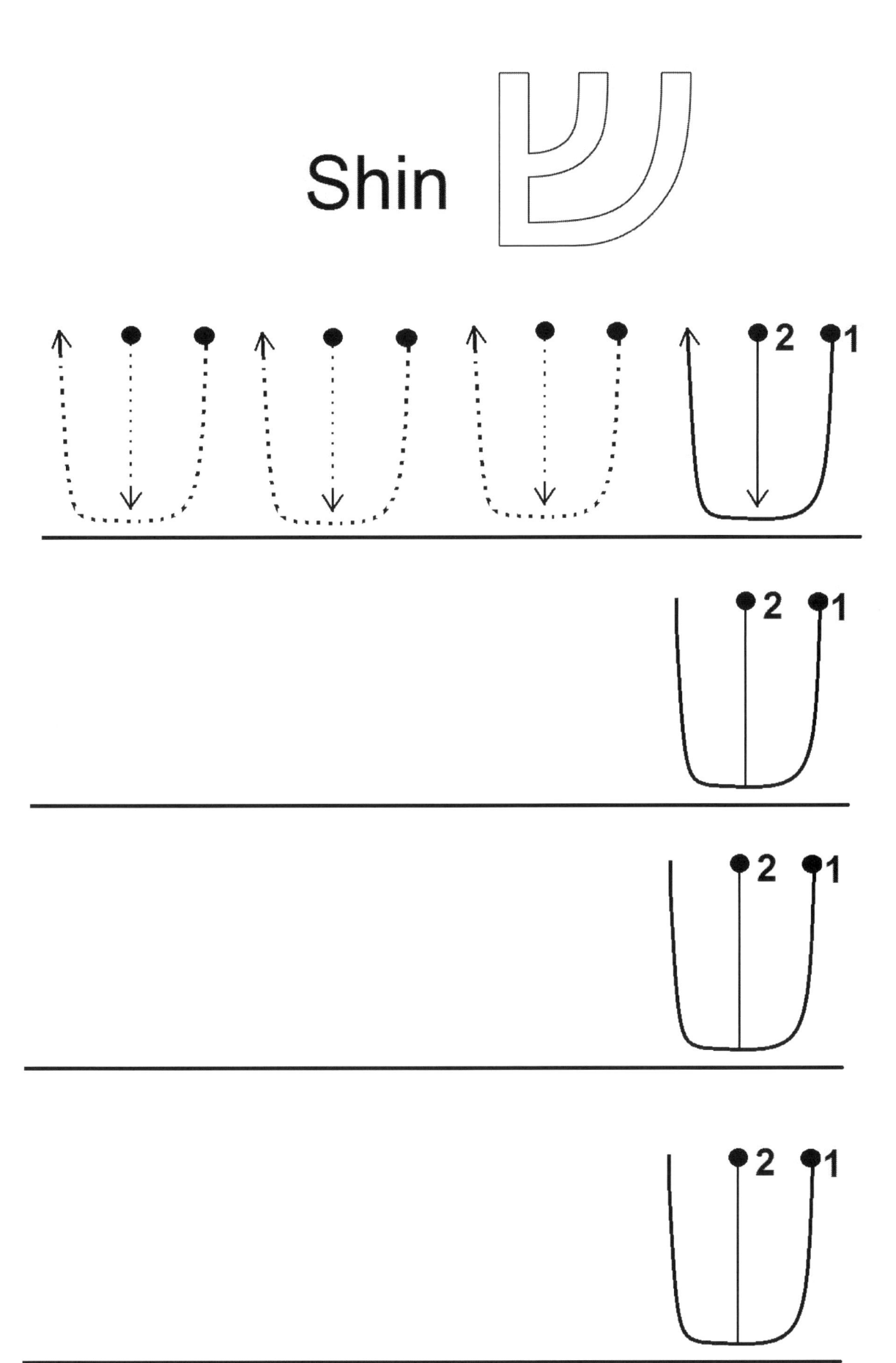

Taf ת

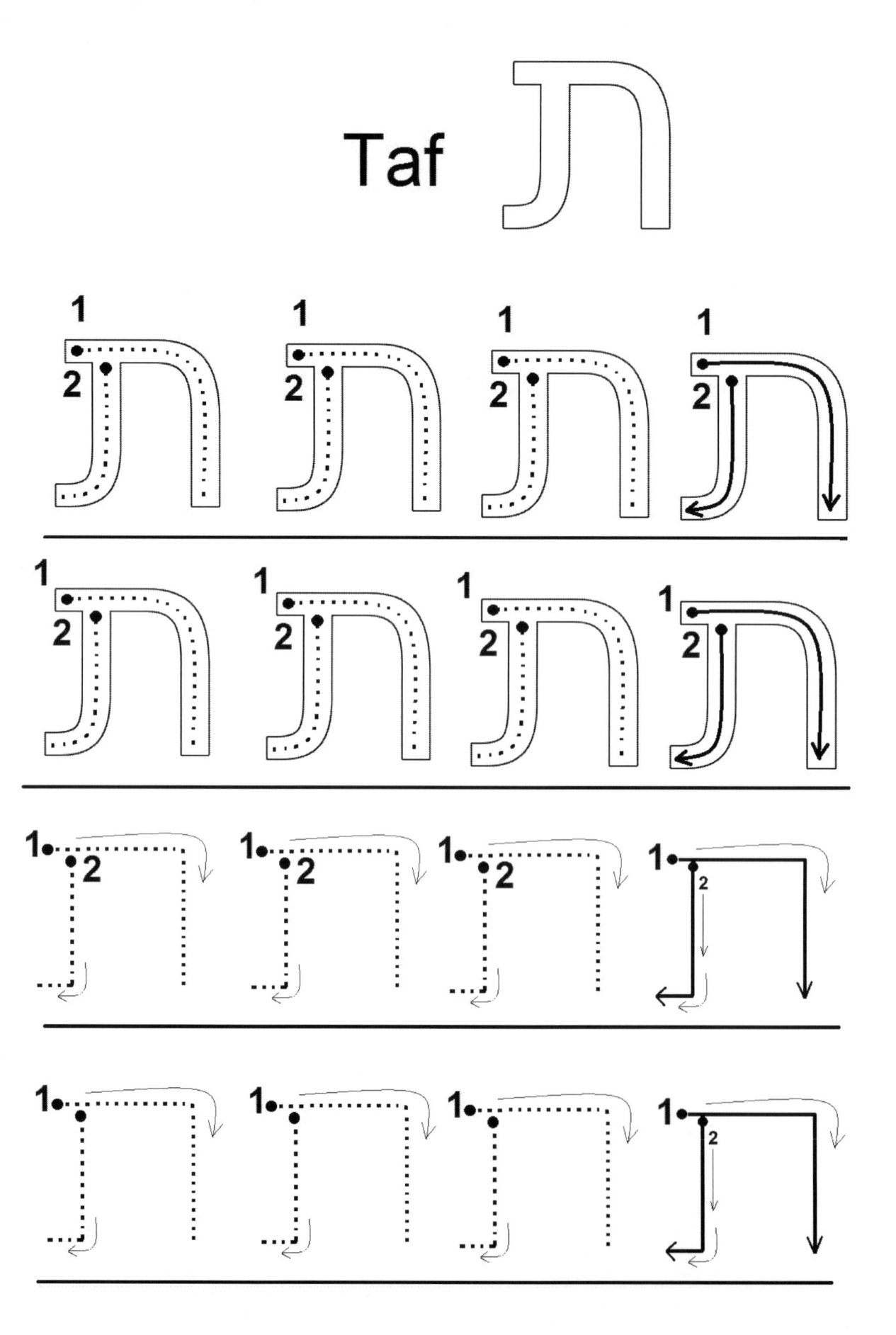

Taf ת

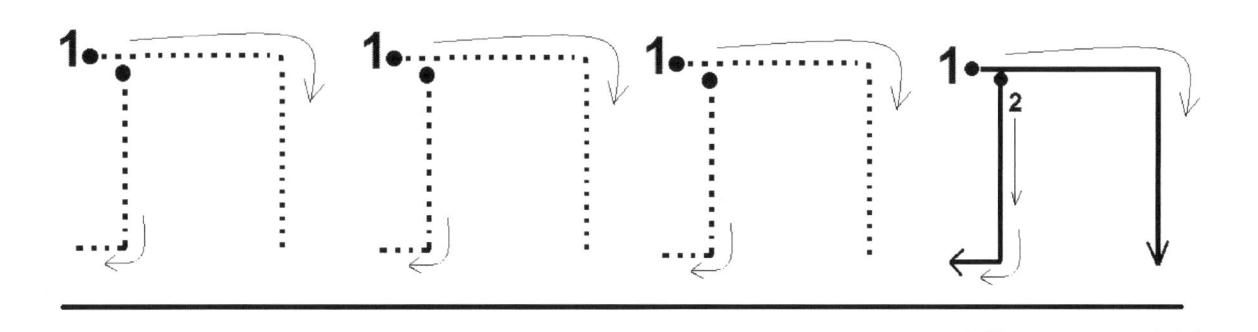

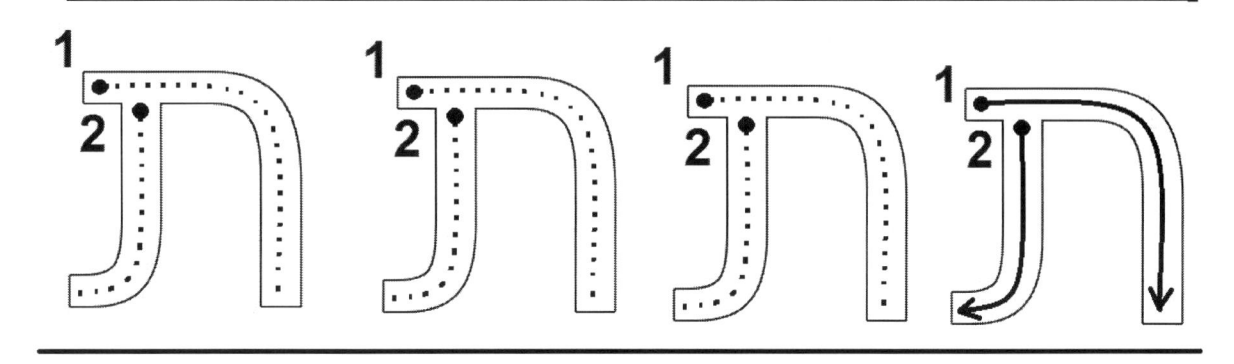

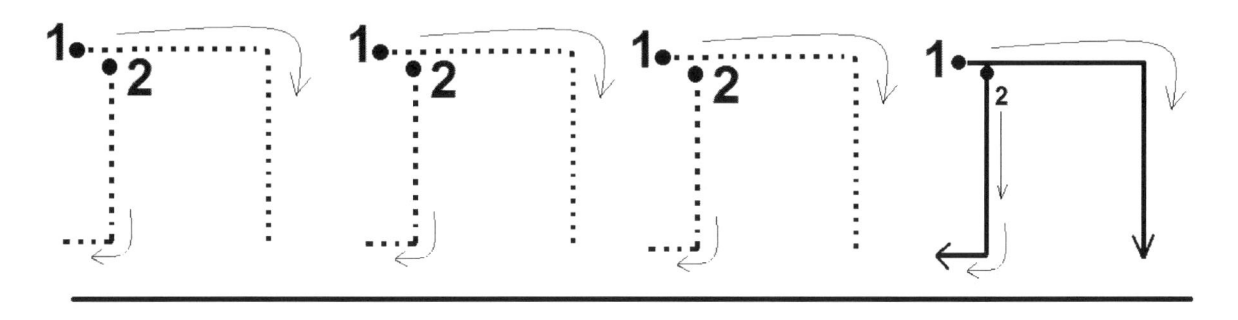

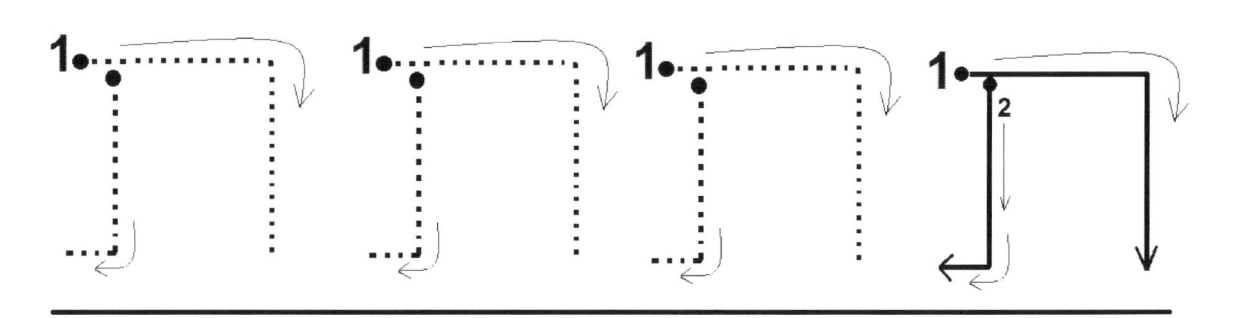

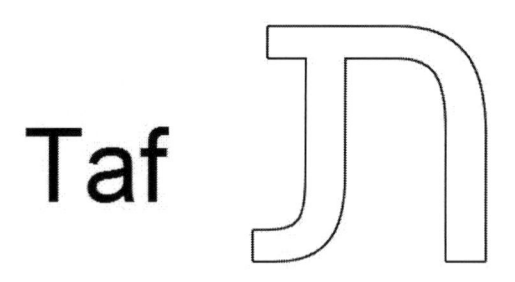

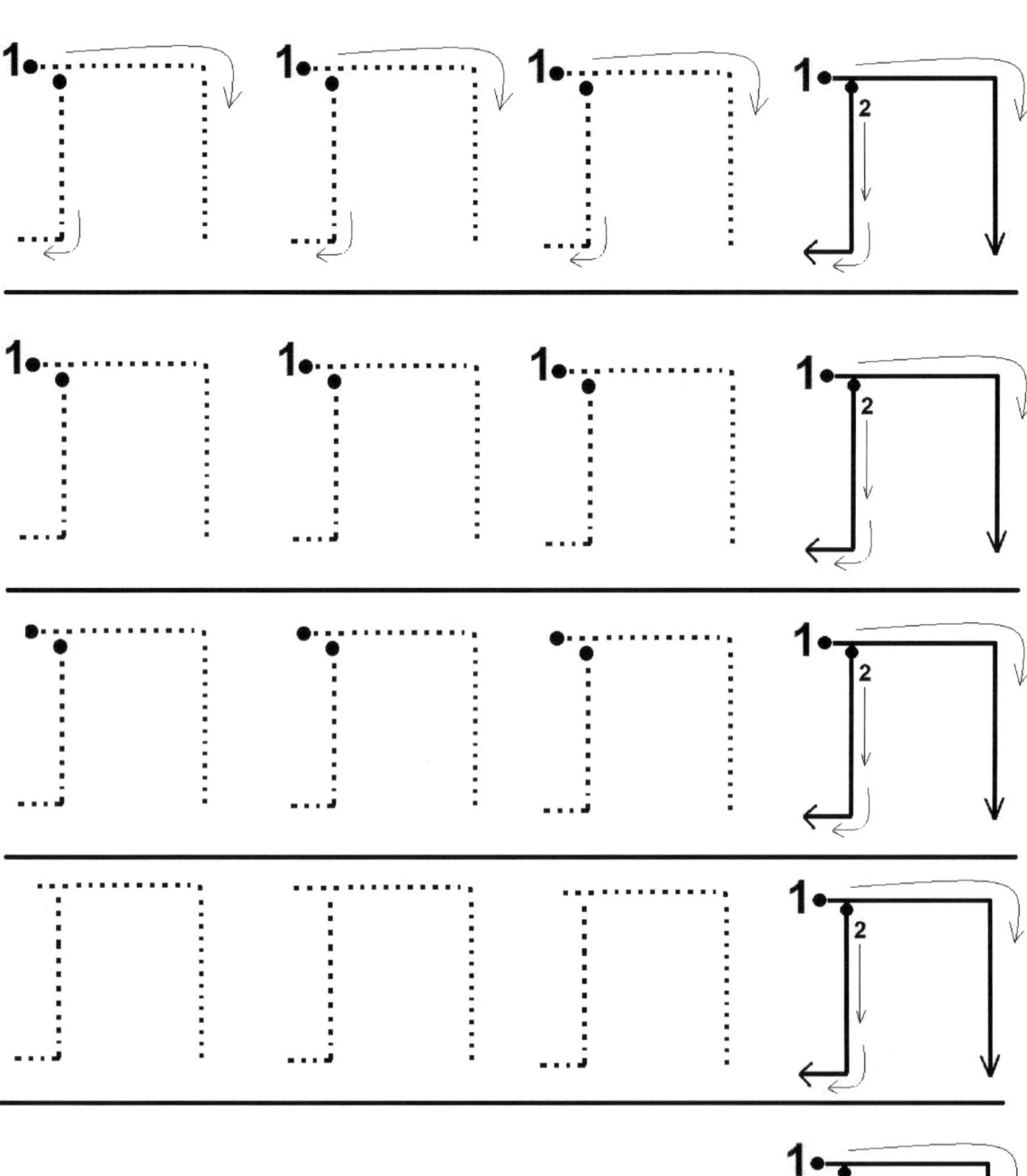

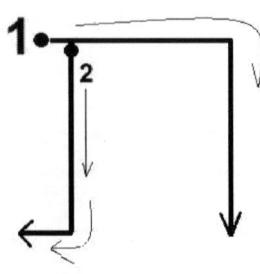

Taf

ד ג ב א
Dalet Gimmel Bet Aleph

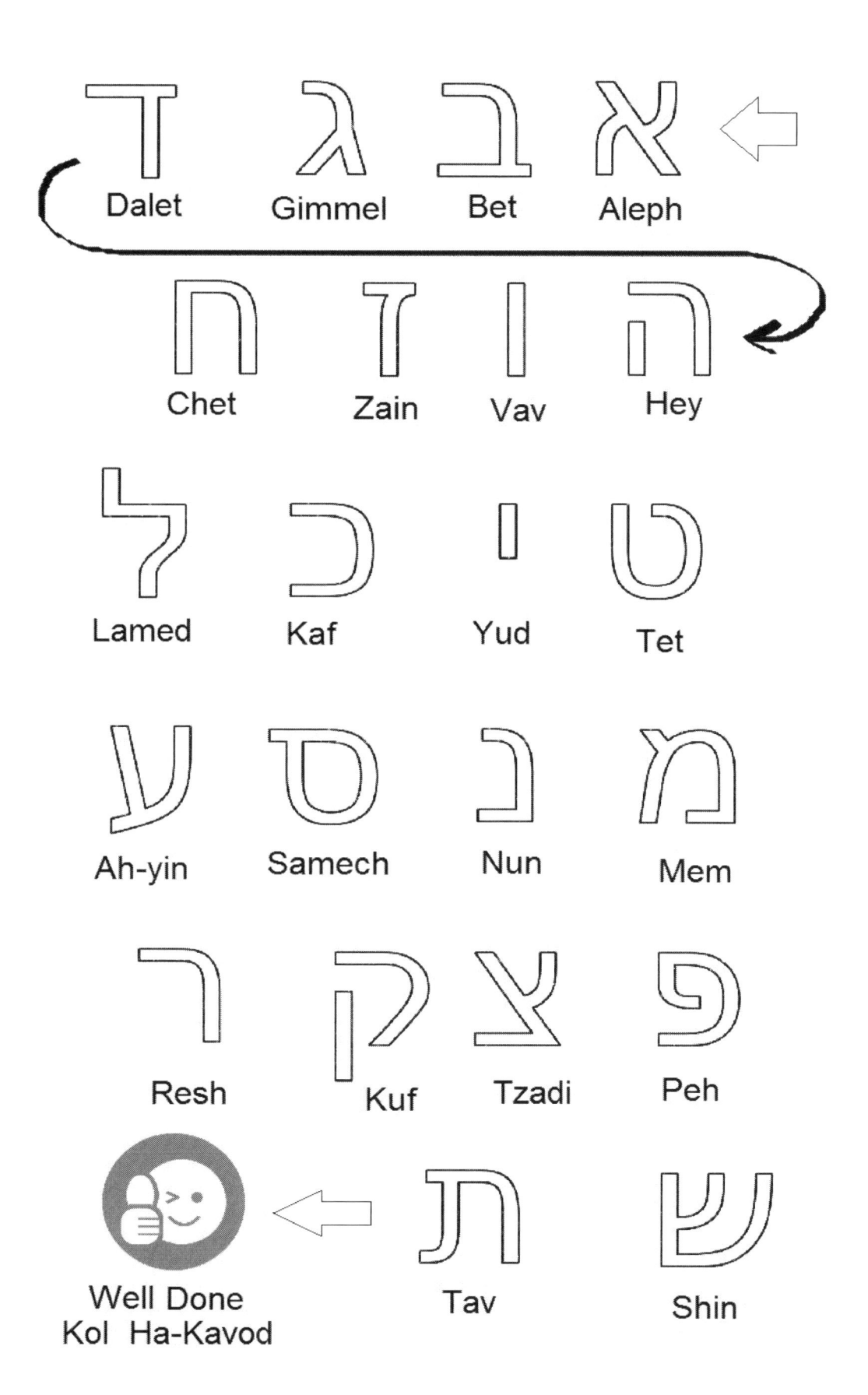

ח ז ו ה
Chet Zain Vav Hey

ל כ י ט
Lamed Kaf Yud Tet

ע ס נ מ
Ah-yin Samech Nun Mem

ר ק צ פ
Resh Kuf Tzadi Peh

ת ש
Well Done Tav Shin
Kol Ha-Kavod

Practice Writing The Hebrew Letters

Kaf ך

Lamed ל

Mem מ

Nun נ

Samech ס

A-yeen ע

Peh פ

Tzadi צ

Koof ק

Resh ר

Shin ש

Taf ת

Final Letters

Like in English, Capital letters are written differently than regular letters (A - a) in Hebrew five letters are written differently when they are at the END of a word. These are called Sofiot.
SOF in Hebrew means END.
The Mem is positioned on the line, like all the other letters, the Kaf, Nun, Peh and Tzadi are written with bottom part below the line.

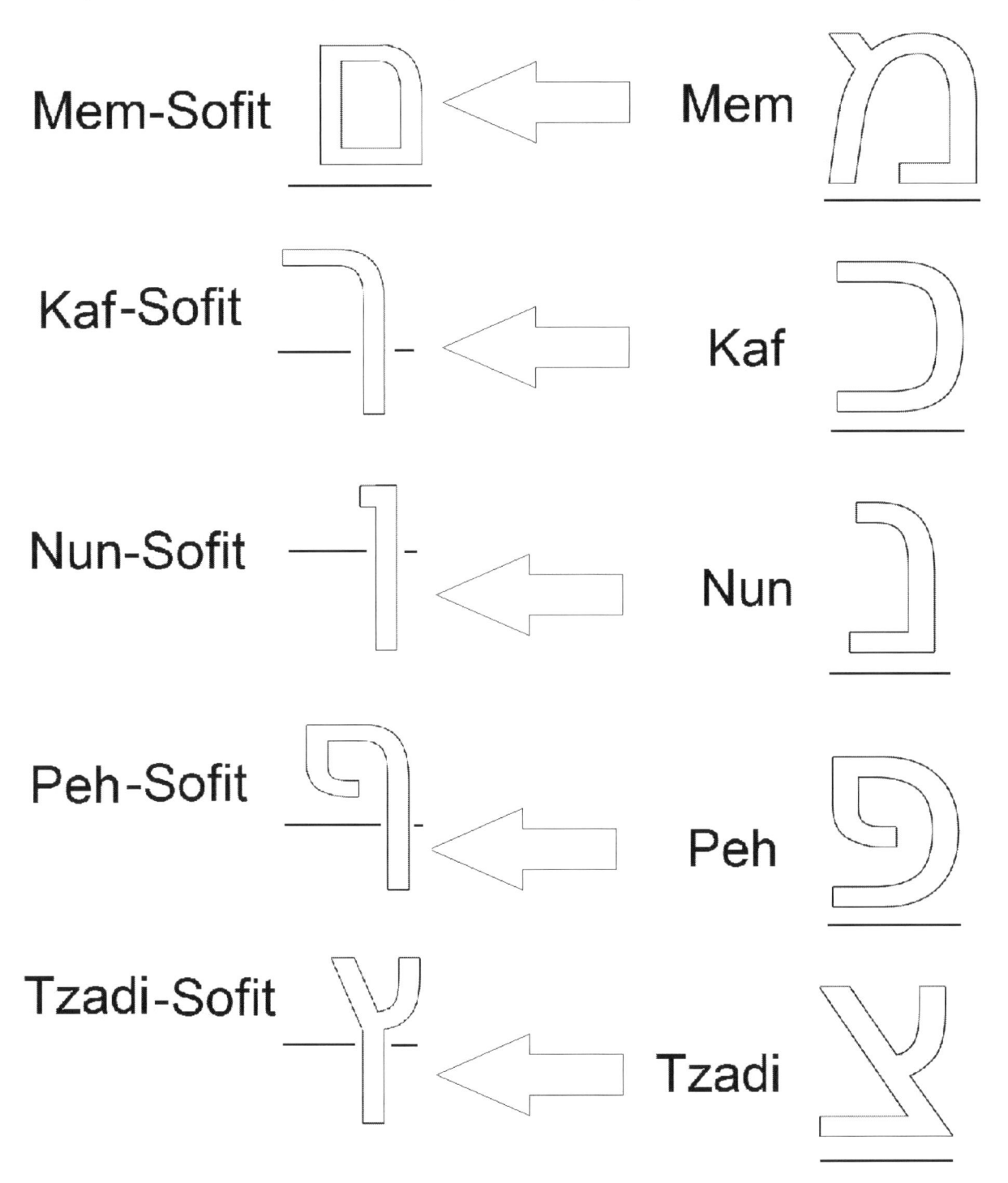

Mem-Sofit	ם	←	Mem מ
Kaf-Sofit	ך	←	Kaf כ
Nun-Sofit	ן	←	Nun נ
Peh-Sofit	ף	←	Peh פ
Tzadi-Sofit	ץ	←	Tzadi צ

Mem-Sofit

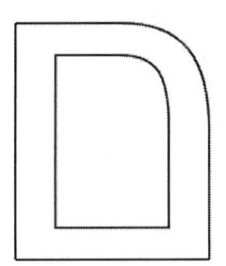

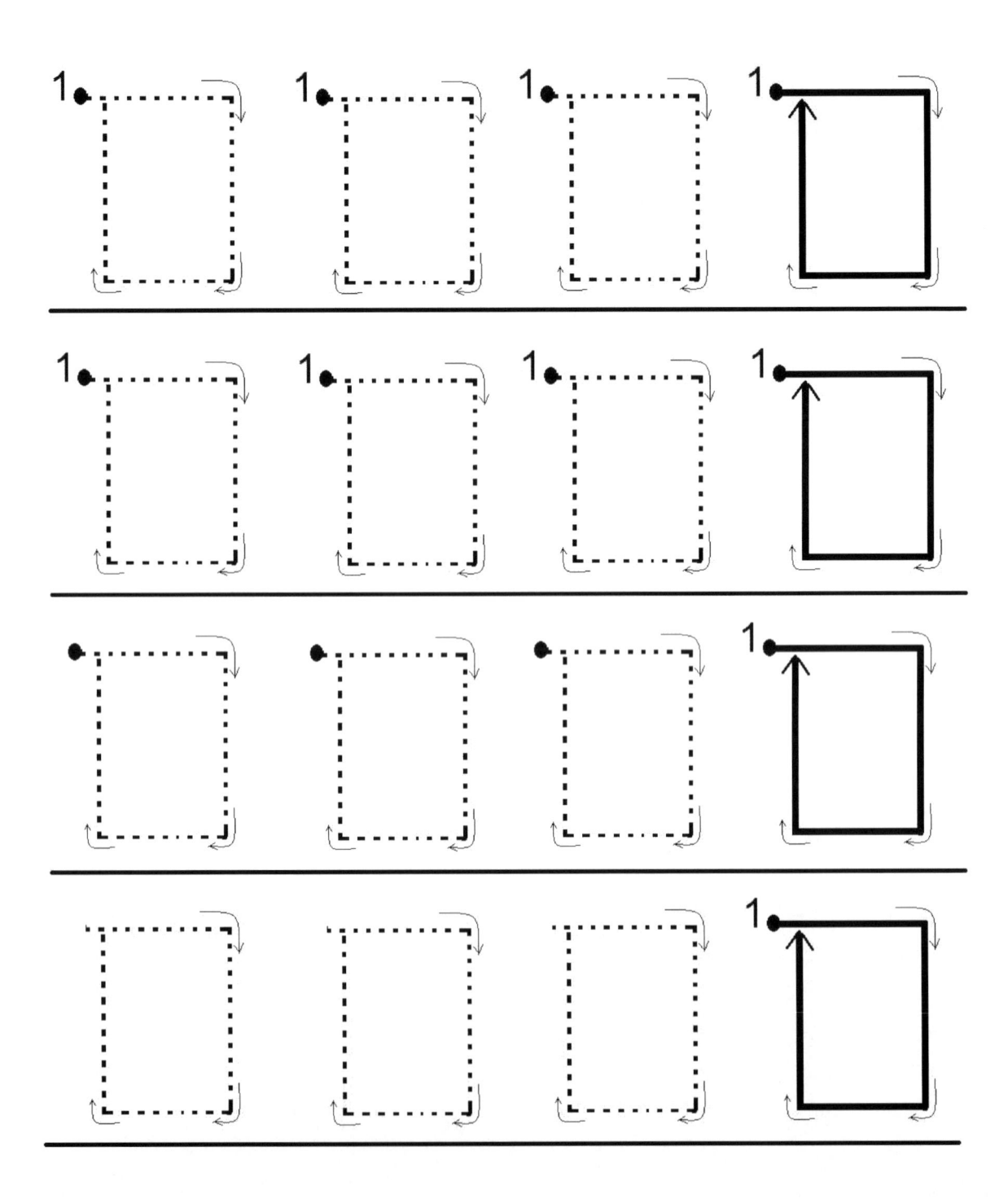

Kaf-Sofit

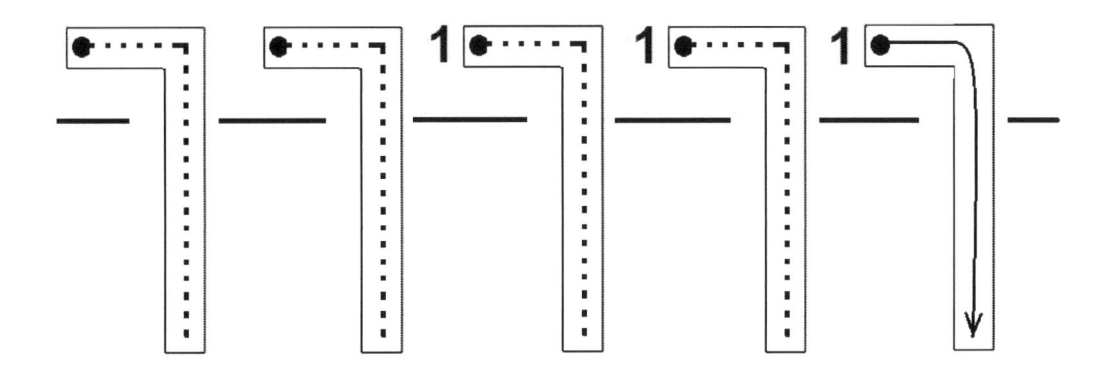

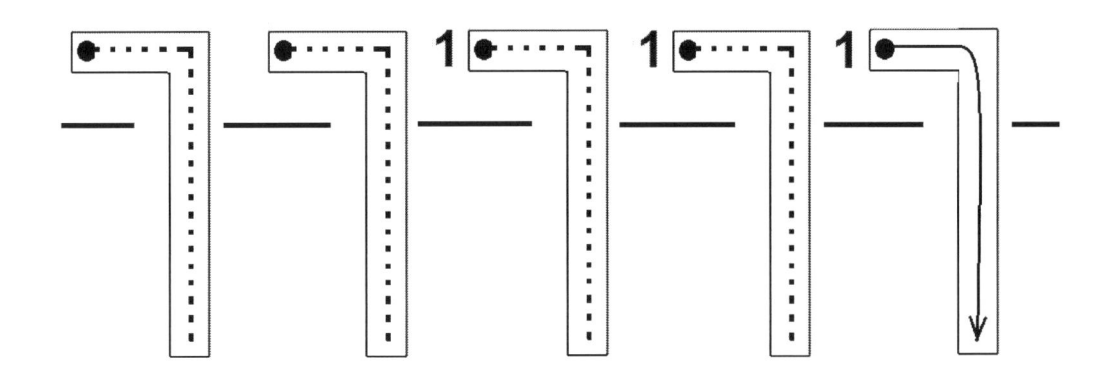

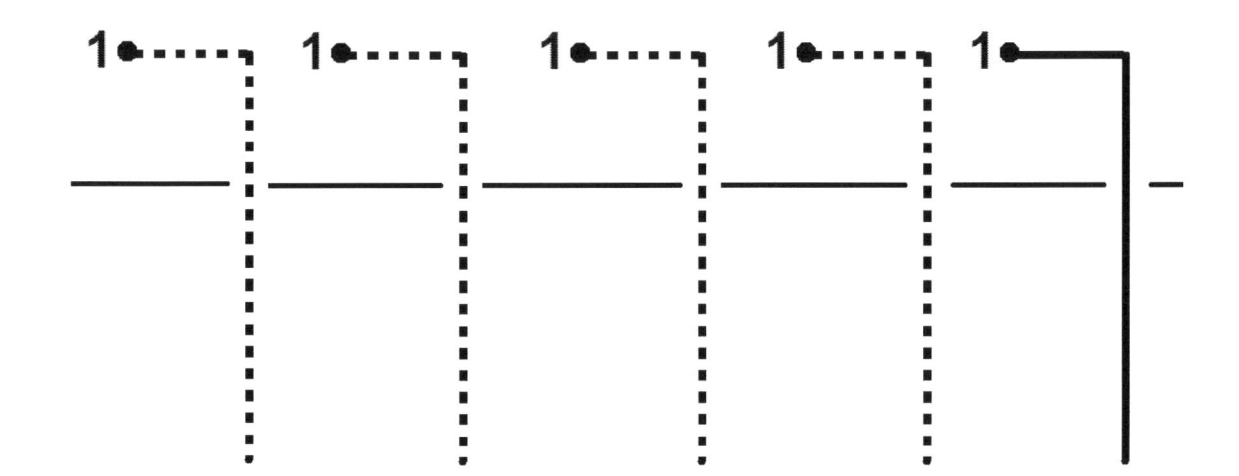

Nun-Sofit

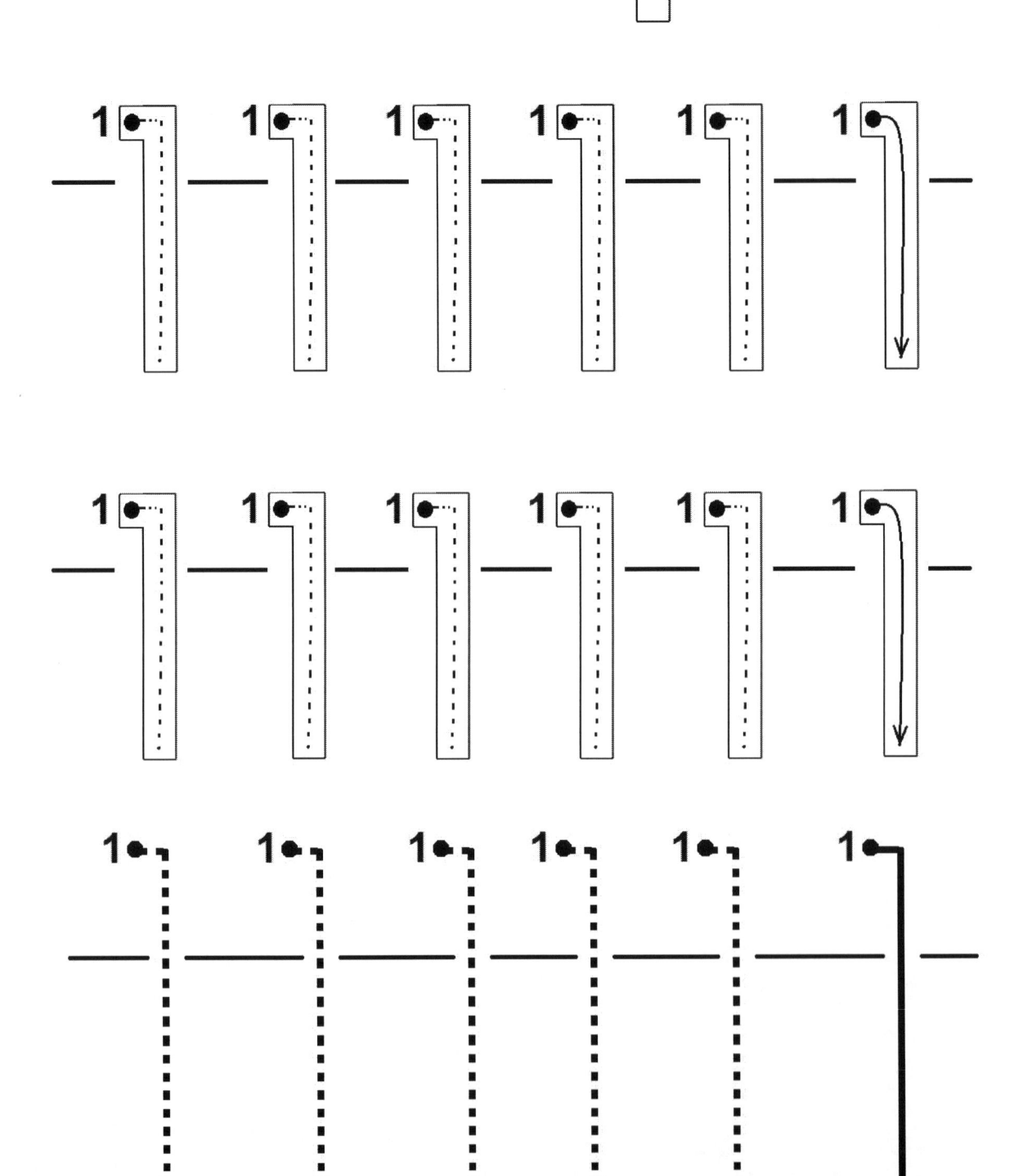

Peh-Sofit

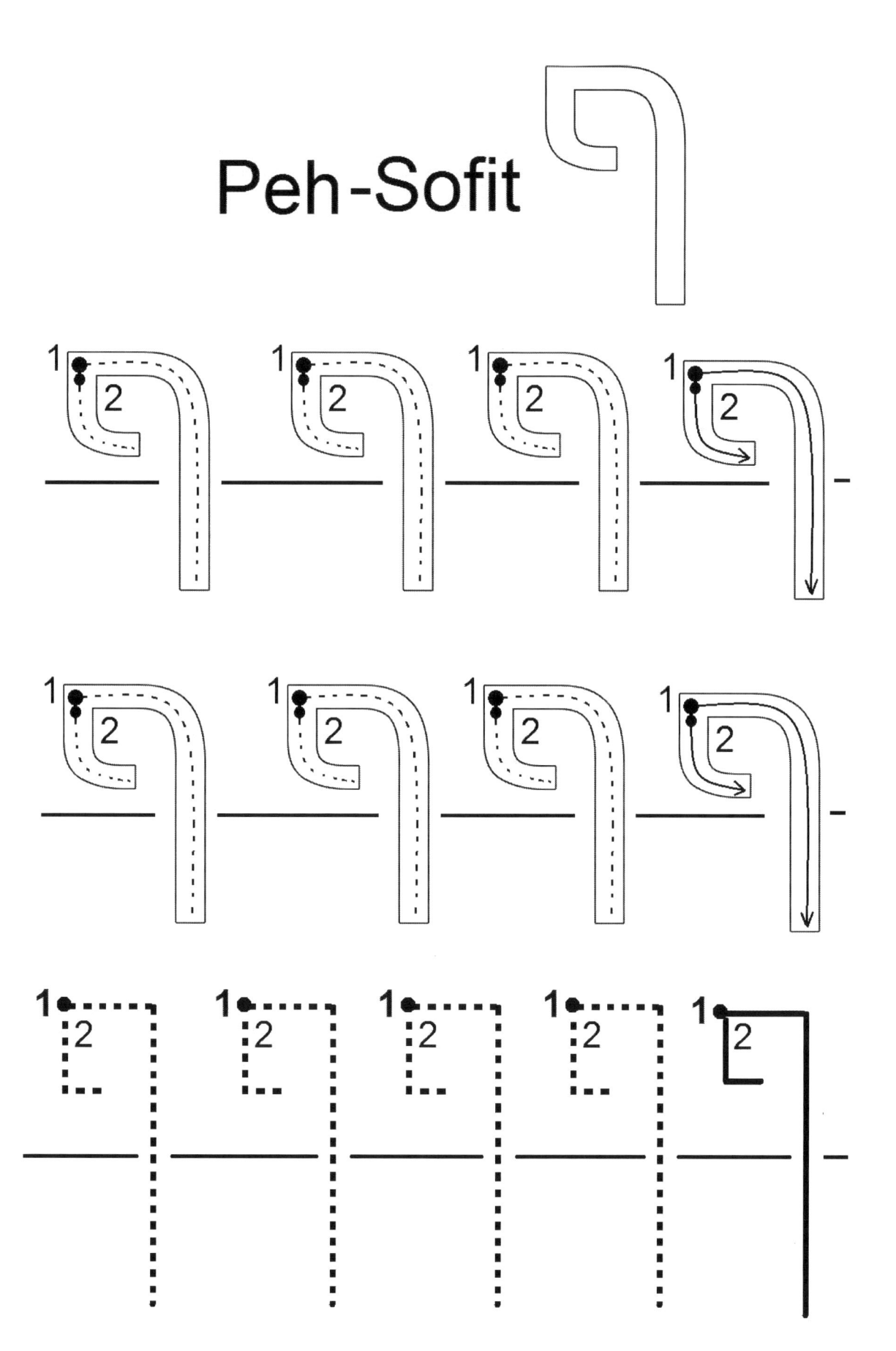

Tzadi-Sofit

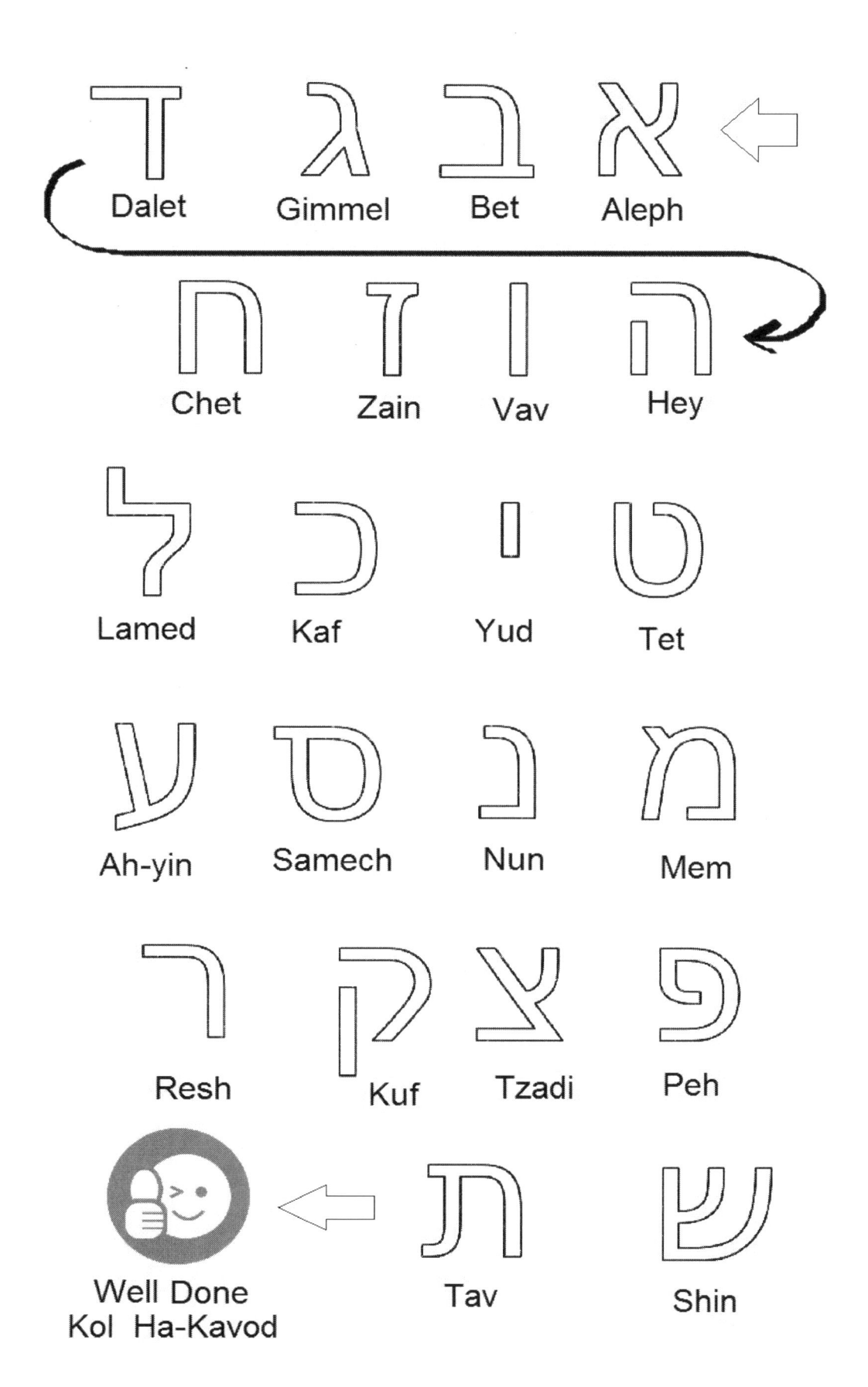

ד Dalet	ג Gimmel	ב Bet	א Aleph
ח Chet	ז Zain	ו Vav	ה Hey
ל Lamed	כ Kaf	י Yud	ט Tet
ע Ah-yin	ס Samech	נ Nun	מ Mem
ר Resh	ק Kuf	צ Tzadi	פ Peh
Well Done Kol Ha-Kavod	ת Tav		ש Shin

Good Luck

בְּהַצְלָחָה

We hope you enjoyed this workbook
Please consider to rate it at Amazon.

Toda Raba - Rachel Mintz

More Hebrew Learning Books

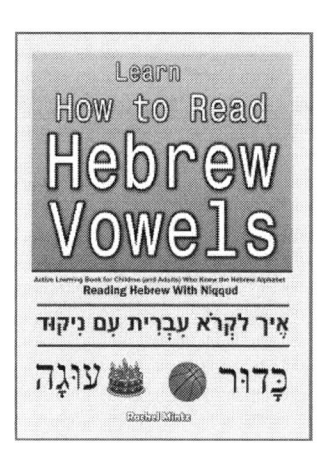

For those who know the Hebrew Aleph-Bet, and want to learn how to read with Hebrew Vowels (Niqqud). Get the best explanations and practice how to pronounce the dots and dashes above and below the Hebrew letters. It will be easier than you might expect!

Younger kids can begin to learn the Aleph-Bet with the coloring book. For those who can write it can go well with this workbook too, learning to write the letters and coloring them for fun.

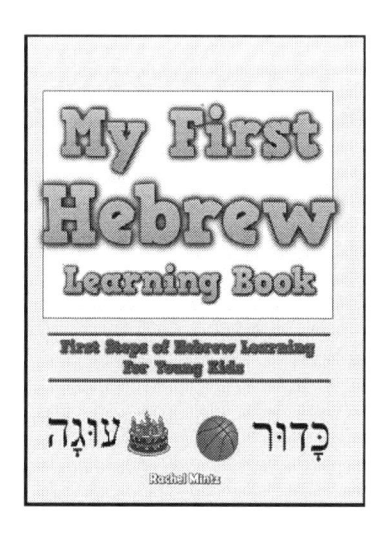

Learning first phrases in Hebrew, learning to count, asking questions in Hebrew (what, where, who?) Learning to to say This, Yes, No, Good Morning.. I Want.. and more. Fun for young kids to practice.

Order Jewish Festivals Fun Books

Fun way to enrich your kids about more Jewish festivals.

Learning the main themes and traditions for each festival with colorful puzzles and creative activities

Learning to count in Hebrew

Fast, and exciting facts book about Israel which will blow your mind!
124 amazing facts you didn't know about Israel.

Think you know Israel?
Take the trivia quiz book about Israel...

Children activity books - Zooming out from extreme close-up images to identify the animal. With toddler rhymes about Piki The Flea.

Short Story Books For Kids

New Books Released

Brains Beats Brawn – Modern Hanukkah Story For Children	A boy deals with bullies at school like Judah Maccabee.
 The Passover Story With Zombies	Passover exodus story with Zombies
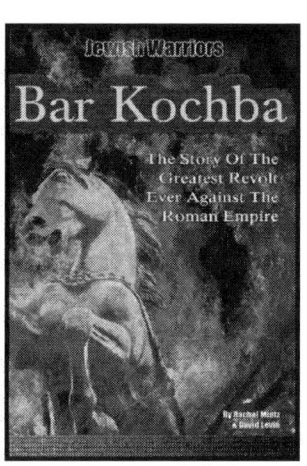 Jewish Warriors: Bar Kochba – The Story Of The Greatest Revolt Ever Against The Roman Empire	The story of the legendary Bar Kochba.
 The Sneaky Tricky Hamantash – A Purim Story	Book for Purim
 Find The Hamantaschen – A Visual Purim Challenge	Search for hiding hamantaschen.
 Judah Maccabee Is Badass	Hillarious facts and funny jokes about Jewish hero.
 The Magic Honey Jar – A Jewish Tale For Rosh Hasharah	A fun Jewish tale for Rosh Hashanah
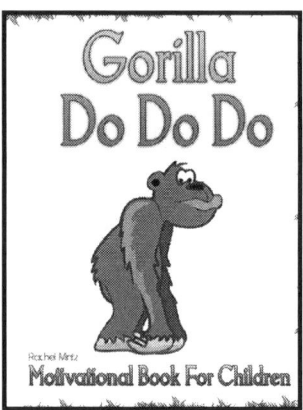 Gorilla Do Do Do – Motivational Book For Children	Motivation book for kids
 The Forest Purim Party	Kids rhyme book illustrated for Purim.
Chungy's Birthday Present	Does happiness come inside a box?
Moses and The Jewish People – The Passover Story in Rhymes	The Passover story in rhymes for kids
 Passover Story – The Boy Who Helped Moses	The Exodus story through a boy's eyes
 Chad Gadya Passover Story	Illustrated story for Passover

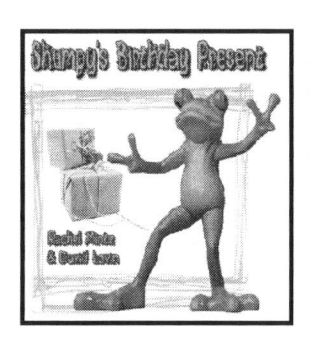

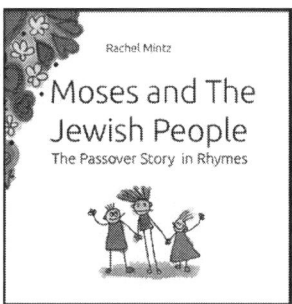

97

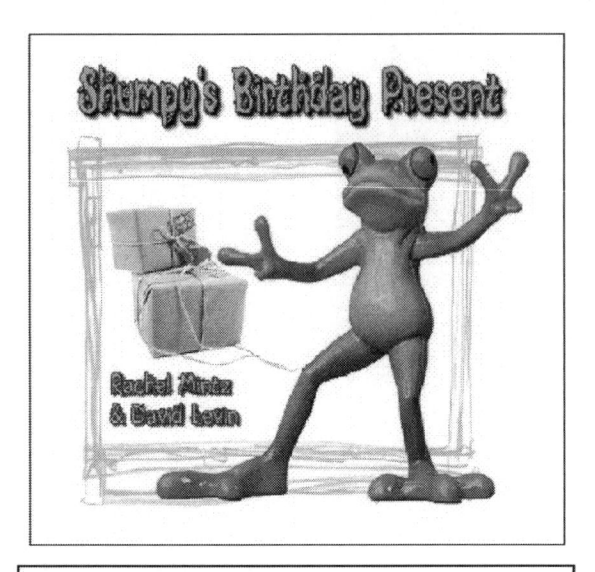

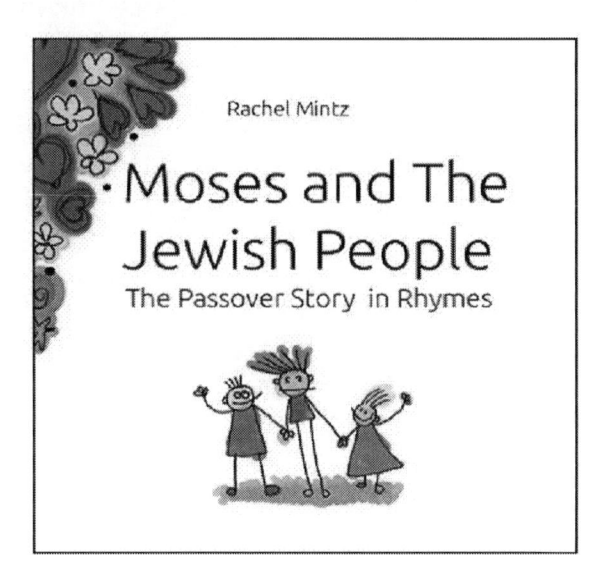

Does happiness come in a box? A book about what is important in life.

The story of Passover told in sweet kids rhymes.

Book with image puzzles of footprints and tracks for young kids to guess ' Who Passed Here?'

Motivational book for children, learning to TAKE ACTION for the things they want to get done.

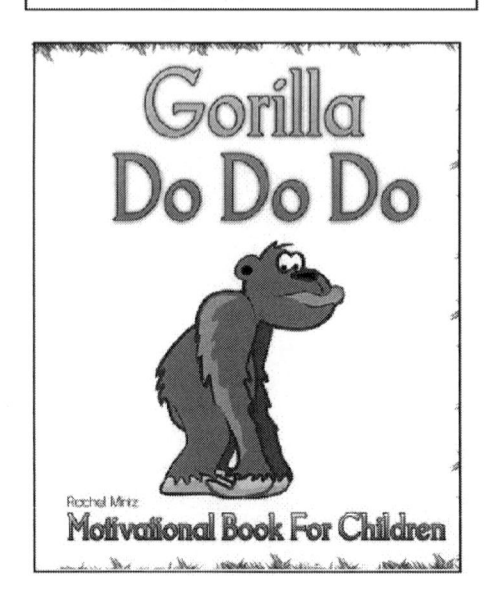

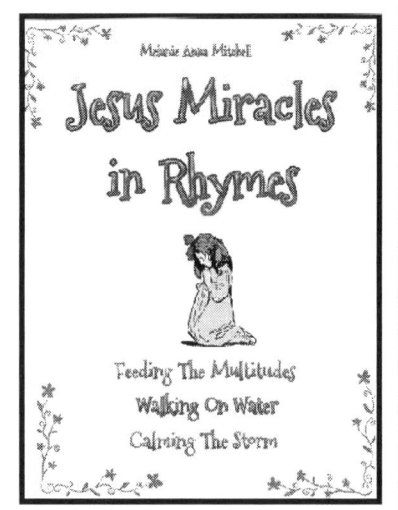

Jesus Miracles in Rhymes
Melanie Anna Mitchell
Feeding The Multitudes
Walking On Water
Calming The Storm

Sweet rhymes for kids

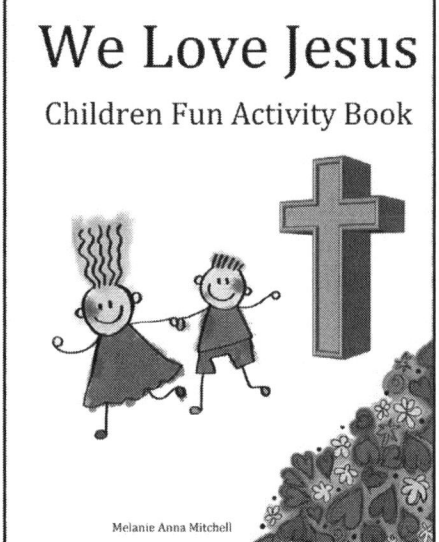

We Love Jesus
Children Fun Activity Book
Melanie Anna Mitchell

THE LARGE CHRISTMAS ACTIVITY BOOK
Puzzles | Mazes | Word search | Find the Difference & More

Fun activities for kids

Zombies Devils Demons Serial Killers Ghosts & Monsters
Rachel Mintz
No Sentence Horror Stories Illustrated For Halloween

Scary, morbid stories for adults

The Smart Owl's 30 Useful English Proverbs For Kids
Rachel Mintz & David Levin

Illustrated proverbs for bright kids

HOW TO PREVENT BABY ACCIDENTS AROUND THE HOUSE
Melanie Anna Mitchell

Over 200 life saving tips!! Must read!

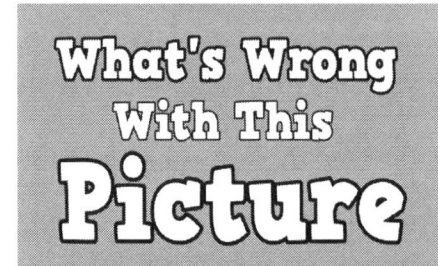

What's Wrong With This Picture
Are You a Keen Observer? Can You Find The Fault?
NO HEADLIGHTS!?
Rachel Mintz

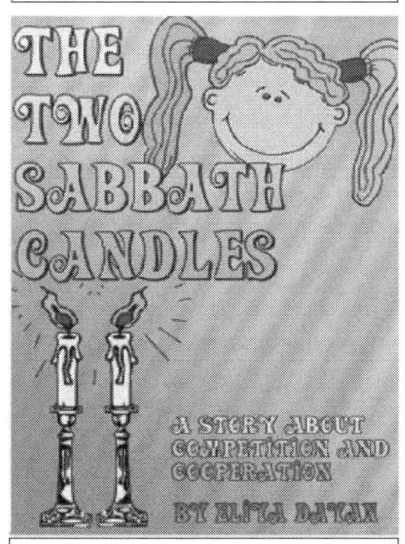

THE TWO SABBATH CANDLES
A STORY ABOUT COMPETITION AND COOPERATION
BY ALIZA DAYAN

Written by a 10 years old girl!

Hanukkah Fun Trivia for The Family
Rachel Mintz & David Levin

Have an educational fun activity for the around the Hanukah candles

Practice Writing The Hebrew Letters

Alef א

Bet ב

Gimel ג

Dalet ד

Hey ה

Vav ו

Zain ז

Chet ח

Tet ט

Yud י

Practice Writing The Hebrew Letters

Kaf ךּ

Lamed ל

Mem מ

Nun נ

Samech ס

A-yeen ע

Peh פ

Tzadi צ

Koof ק

Resh ר

Shin ש

Taf ת

Practice Writing The Hebrew Letters

Alef
Bet
Gimel
Dalet
Hev
Vav
Zain
Chet
Tet
Yud
Kaf
Lamed
Mem
Nun
Samech
A-yeen
Peh
Tzadi
Koof
Resh
Shin
Taf

Practice Writing The Hebrew Letters

Alef
_____
Bet
_____
Gimel
_____
Dalet
_____
Hev
_____
Vav
_____
Zain
_____
Chet
_____
Tet
_____
Yud
_____
Kaf
_____
Lamed
_____
Mem
_____
Nun
_____
Samech
_____
A-yeen
_____
Peh
_____
Tzadi
_____
Koof
_____
Resh
_____
Shin
_____
Taf
_____

Practice Writing The Hebrew Letters

Alef

Bet

Gimel

Dalet

Hev

Vav

Zain

Chet

Tet

Yud

Kaf

Lamed

Mem

Nun

Samech

A-yeen

Peh

Tzadi

Koof

Resh

Shin

Taf

Write Your Name in Hebrew

Rachel = רחל

Shalom = שלום

Israel = ישראל

Good Luck

בְּהַצְלָחָה

We hope you enjoyed this workbook
Please consider to rate it at Amazon.

Toda Raba - Rachel Mintz

Printed in Great Britain
by Amazon